A Trace in the Sky

Éditions Favre SA

Head Office	Paris Office
29, rue de Bourg	12, rue Duguay-Trouin
CH-1002 Lausanne	F-75006 Paris
Tel.: 021/312 17 17	Tel.: 01 42 22 01 90
Fax: 021/320 50 59	Fax: 01 42 22 01 90
lausanne@editionsfavre.com	paris@editionsfavre.com

Original edition (French):
copyright registered in Switzerland in November 2005

Cover photo: © Jules Verne Aventures/www.jva.fr/A. Childéric

Translation: Nadine Martinat

Cover: MGraphic, J.-P. Piantanida
Page setting: Marie-Hélène Marquis

ISBN: 978-2-8289-1013-6

© 2008 by Bertrand Piccard

Bertrand Piccard

A Trace in the Sky

FAVRE

CONTENTS

FOREWORD

A BALLOON LIFTING OFF in the icy winter sky, a balloon going up, beyond the mountains, and disappearing. We were all like kids watching Piccard and his colleague rise in the air and search for the winds, intending to do a trip round the world.

It was as simple as Icarus' dream. Like a page taken from a Jules Verne novel. Like a volatile, elegant fabric of madness detaching itself from the rags of our gravity.

Piccard's adventure isn't a technical one, or at least not only a technical one. First of all, it is a spiritual adventure. Piccard isn't a Passepartout a Phileas Fogg. He's like Saint-Exupéry overflying the desert. His vision of the world is that of the Little Prince.

Whether he succeeds or not is of secondary importance. At least he will have tried, unlike us, Earthlings. Men are not my fellow creatures, said one of Malraux's characters. They watch me and judge me. My fellow creatures are those who love me and don't watch me.

One would like to think of Piccard as Tchang's scarf, lost among the rocks, which draws Hergé's hero, Tintin, into a search for the absolute. Not for the adventure in itself, but for the fraternity of men.

Let us wish Bertrand Piccard a fair journey. Let us wish for the Heavens, in all meanings of the term, to be on his side.

Pascal Décaillet, *Radio Journalist*

I tried everything to stop the course of time.
Marking the walls and the bark of trees
With words I no longer remember
In my childhood memories;
With all my strength and perseverance
I truly hoped to preserve my innocence;
But walls have collapsed and trees have grown.
I am searching for a resemblance
in my childhood photographs,
But you cannot shield remembrance
from this merciless flow.
Living always in the present
Is the only way to stop the course of time.

LIVE FROM THE SKY

These fleeting instants I wanted to last forever…

I AM VERY LONELY WHEN I FLY. Of course, this type of solitude encourages concentration, a certain form of consciousness, and above all, self-awareness at all times. But after the landing, it's just one more obstacle. When people ask me to tell them what the experience was like, I can only reconstruct it in snatches: I am no longer living it out. This is why, during my most intense experiences, I've sometimes kept at the back of my mind a record of what I'd be saying later. One day, I felt the need to gather in a book all these impressions gathered LIVE from the sky. From now on, I would be less lonely when flying.

The intensity of my impressions depends on the type of experience and the frame of mind I am in. My different chapters, unfolding like 'tales from the sky', are therefore not necessarily equal or written in a chronological order. Yet there is a main thread: the impressions, the atmosphere, and a desire to hold back those fleeting instants which I wanted to be eternal.

Indeed, our whole life is made of a few moments of grace, like snapshots that leave a permanent impression on you. They make you see, through those rare moments of awakening, that there is another state of consciousness. This book's sole aim is to make readers want to live their existence like a great adventure; to discover the special moments which punctuate it, and explore personally these subtle and magical states which suddenly add a new dimension to your life.

If this aim is achieved, then I shall feel less lonely when flying.

ARIADNE'S THREAD

My greatest wish was to stop the course of time

IF THE INFLUENCE EXPLORERS have had over the first years of my life could be measured in pages, this chapter would take up most of the book. But my adult words can no longer convey what I felt as a child, that broad impression which remains after you've experienced something quintessential. All I can do is write a few lines, trying to recall that natural, limpid, naïve, muffled atmosphere, close to the source, which you can sometimes recall if you try long enough.

In the haze of my earliest childhood memories, I can see myself going upstairs and running towards my grandfather sitting in his armchair. I was three or four. He was the man who had made the first trip into the stratosphere, who had gone furthest away from the Earth, who had invented the pressurised cabin (now used in most aeroplanes, and which NASA classified as the first space capsule). His ascents in 1931 and 1932 had given as much to talk about in their days as the first landing on the Moon would do later, overshadowing his other inventions in a variety of scientific fields.

Indeed, apart from being the first man to have seen the curvature of the Earth with his own eyes, he had also discovered Uranium 235, which he had then called Actinuran. And he had built the most reliable seismograph and the most precise scales of the time. He was an all-round scientist and his legendary exactness had caused him to be nicknamed 'extra decimal'.

But who were those scientists pictured around him at the Solvay Institute, whom everybody admired? I didn't know they were called Marie Curie, Albert Einstein, Max Planck, Niels Bohr or that they had discovered the laws of modern physics. I had no idea what that meant, of course. Nor did I know about this Einstein who had sent him a touching letter of thanks. Later, I would learn that at the time of his first publications on the theory of relativity, Einstein had been strongly attacked by other physicists, and that it was one of my grandfather's experiments, carried out from a balloon, which had proved the exactitude of the hypotheses on the speed of light.

I also wondered why so many people were telling me that they felt honoured to have met my grandfather, that they would never forget his tall slightly stooping figure, his charisma and his modesty; or that they had once caught sight of him while walking in the streets of Brussels, Paris or Lausanne, but had not dared approach him.

In the laboratory, where I was sometimes allowed, I could play with a model of the bathyscaphe. That was another of my grandfather's creations, based on the principle of the stratospheric balloon but designed to explore ocean trenches. For me, it was just one more toy, but I knew I had better not break it! It was thanks to this strange machine that my grandfather was now known as the man who had made both the highest ascent and the lowest descent ever.

Hergé used him as a model to draw his Professor Calculus. The stratosphere had propelled him into history and Tintin albums had turned him into a legend. But he was my grandfather and I found it all very normal.

Just as I found it perfectly normal for my father to have dived with a bathyscaphe into the deepest ocean trench, or to have built the first tourist sub-marine in the world. A mesoscaphe for forty passengers, which I would often watch from the terrace of our apartment as it left for a dive. Jules Verne was no science-fiction to me, my daily life at home seemed to be taken straight out of his books.

When I went to the cinema with my father to see *Twenty Thousand Leagues Under the Sea*, I sat next to Captain Nemo, the real one, mine. How could a kid like me see it otherwise? For me, there was nothing strange in seeing my father on television, or side by side with the most important people in the world, or receiving a medal from the President of the United States, that's what I'd been used to from early childhood.

But when Hermann Geiger, the pilot known for his trips to the glaciers, came to fetch us from our holiday chalet in a helicopter, the six-year old child that I was then made his first step into the adult world of aeronautics. Of course, I had already flown over the Atlantic in a DC7 at the age of one, I had been over California in a helicopter, and I had always played with model planes, but that day I really felt I was flying. A few days later, Geiger took us round the Matterhorn in a Piper. My first 13,000 ft… and the first time I suffered air sickness. I can still see the pilot opening a valve to let some fresh air in on my face. This was the real stuff, I was flying, and with one of the pioneers who had shaped modern aviation. When Hermann Geiger died after a crash during a training session at Sion airfield, I burst into tears. Cursing the pilot of the second aircraft – although he had not caused the accident, I said he had 'killed my hero', the man who had really made me discover the third dimension. My dreams were shattered as I realised that, despite all its magic, there were risks inherent in flying.

Then, evolving between model aeroplanes and aviation books, between dives in the mesoscaphe and intercontinental flights, I was lucky enough to spend two years in Florida, near Cape Kennedy, in the full midst of the Apollo launches. Above all, I was lucky because, although I was ten, my parents had me take part in everything they could. This is why I often went along with my father to the Palm Beach dock where he was adding the finishing touches to his second mesoscaphe. He had created it for the American Grumman company to explore the Gulf Stream, that warm current which crosses the Atlantic. I even painted a tiny portion of the hull and felt very involved in this oceanographical mission!

My most vivid memory of that one-month expedition is the departure itself: my mother, my brother, my sister and I escorting the submarine, running along the dike as far as possible to follow the tug-boat going to open sea. I had asked my father to take a walkie-talkie with him, and we could hear his voice getting weaker and weaker until interference covered our emotion.

For thirty days, we would mark the submarine's position on the map with a red dot, after getting regular reports from the escort ship. Then there was the triumphant arrival in New York, under jets of water spouting from the fire boats celebrating the return of the expedition, with the Statue of Liberty in the background. For us, this was just dad's return. But journalists were fighting over him, and during a whole month spent near New York we were hardly able to see him at all. I only got truly reconciled with that mission when my father let me write a short chapter in the book about his expedition!

This was also the time when I discovered and marvelled at the fascinating world of advanced space technology, under the guidance of Wernher von Braun, the father of the NASA lunar programme, and Bill Ellsworth, head of public relations at Grumman, builder of the lunar module. Two people I shall never forget. They were able to draw a bridge between a child's world and science, answering all my questions with great attention. They even got me the best places to watch six launches! From Apollo 7 to Apollo 12 I watched the rockets take off, from the security enclosures reserved for the

NASA staff or from the VIP stalls, mixing with heads of state from the entire world. In fact, that caused a bit of a fuss because the son of a NASA director had been refused access due to his tender age... the same as mine! As for Apollo 11, I watched the departure to the Moon next to Peter von Braun, who was also about 11. I have kept this memorable countdown on a precious tape:

'15 seconds, passing on channel, 12, 11, 10, 9, ignition sequence start, 6, 5, 4, 3, 2, 1, 0, all engines running, lift off, lift off Apollo 11'

The Earth was trembling under the reactors of the Saturn V rocket, so were our hearts. We were living one of the most fabulous moments of history: amidst a great storm of fire, some astronauts were going to walk on the Moon! And here we were, Peter and I, all eyes and ears. His father was in the act of reaching his ultimate goal in life, and yet, the night before, he had found time to make sure I could go with his son. When returning from the traditional cocktail party that precedes every launch, he had put me to bed with his children, already asleep, so that I could reach the launch pad more rapidly. I met Peter when he woke up wondering who was asleep next to him! His anguished cry "Mum, there is a boy in my bed!" amused our parents an awful lot.

Cape Kennedy is much more to me than building halls, radar rooms and launch pads: I had the opportunity to discover the men who forged this formidable part of history and to record, deep in my memory, in the hazy mist of a child's vision, some touching words and gestures. I can see Wernher von Braun, again, being persuaded to come and see my bedroom full of posters of rockets, and replying naturally to all my questions on a small tape recorder; it was on my games table that he signed the copy of the *World History of Astronautics* which my father had given me that day. He even confessed that it was after attending one of my grandfather's lectures as a student that he had made the wish to send a rocket to the Moon with people on board. Some dreams come true!

I also met Eugène Cernan, the last man to walk on the Moon, Walter Cunningham, David Scott, John Young, from the Apollo programme, all so willing to sign the postcards I would send to my school friends back in Switzerland. And William Anders, who came to Palm Beach to see my father's mesoscaphe: it was he who read the beginning of the Book of Genesis on Christmas Eve, with Bormann and Lowell, from the Apollo 8 in lunar orbit: "In the beginning, God created the heaven and the earth…" While watching the Earth rise from the Moon this crew was sending, beyond all dogmas and religious barriers, a simple believer's message to billions of humans.

There was James Lowell, the future captain of Apollo 13, reporting live on the launching of Apollo 9. Then, Charles Lindbergh, the North Atlantic hero, who had almost retired from the public arena towards the end of his life.

Much later, when I saw the superb film *The Right Stuff*, my heart was pounding as I recognised the astronauts from the Mercury programme: Scott Carpenter, with whom I had celebrated my twelfth birthday in California, Walter Shirra, Alan Sheppard, John Glenn, who had laughingly let themselves be photographed with me, in many NASA receptions, amused by that child with great big eyes wanting to grasp everything at once.

I was far from guessing that, even much later, after the successful trip around the world in a balloon, a good number of my heroes would attend a lecture which I was giving in Los Angeles for the Society of Experimental Test Pilots. After the standing ovation which they gave me to show that they now regarded me as one of them, a 70-year-old man approached me and said almost timidly:

"My name is Scott Carpenter, do you recognise me?"

But out of all the autographs I proudly collected at Cape Kennedy, the one which would probably move me most, even thirty years on, was written by Don Eisele, from Apollo 7, on the photo of a lunar module in orbit:

'Good luck, Bertrand.'

Indeed, I am very lucky. I've had the incredible chance to live historical events, to meet some extraordinary people, to be enriched by unique experiences, but I think that my greatest luck was that my parents always treated me like a 'responsible person'. I never got those awful replies so often given to children:

"Don't look for an explanation; you're too young to understand; you're worrying yourself too much!"

On the contrary, I was given total freedom to question things. For example, when I saw the astronauts having to face retirement after those moments of glory, reduced to living in the past after having paraded in Broadway under a shower of confetti. Or, when I learned that 20th century science had not been able to cure Wernher von Braun's cancer. When I confronted, in fact, the innocent realm of childhood with everyday reality, I often screamed 'why?' Why is it that man can fly, that he can walk on the Moon, but that he doesn't even know the meaning of his life on Earth. Why make science leap so far ahead, towards the outer world, when his own inner world is even more obscure to him than the dark side of the Moon?

I lived my life very intensely while in America, remembering almost every detail, with the fascination of a child who still thinks that life is easy. But, although I then wanted to be an astronaut, of course, I still felt that a page of History was being turned: nothing would be the same ever again, 'everything' had been done. Everything was there, in front of me, in the big hall of the National Air and Space Museum in Washington, from the Wright Brothers' first aircraft to the Apollo 11 capsule, and I dreamily wondered what might still be left for my life. We had walked on the Moon and, from now on, astronauts would be scientists, not pioneers.

The power of computers had begun to surpass that of brains and I thought that, in the future, adventures would be technological ones, not human ones.

For a long time, I felt intensely nostalgic about an extraordinary epic which I would not live again… In my eyes, aviation had reached its limits and yet I still wanted to live intensely. I also felt that the naivety of a child's world was not going to resist much longer against crude reality. I think that my greatest wish then was to try and stop the course of time, to prolong such a natural and spellbinding atmosphere; that would probably explain the beginning of the quest I was to undertake later in order to get a little closer to the psyche and spirituality of man. Perhaps I sensed, without being aware of it, that what really matters isn't so much the events as such but the way you live them. The deep consciousness of a detail has far more influence over an individual than the automatic and unconscious vision of his daily life. This is why even a trivial incident can seem to have been longer and more intense than a whole day; it may even be the only thing you'll remember from a particular year… Beyond their naivety, children seem to be closer to the source of consciousness. Could this be the reason why time feels slower to them than to adults? Every detail being recorded more deeply, it leaves a more durable mark on them. We have a lot to learn from children at that level. Now, when I find myself searching deep into the eyes of a baby, I often experience a strong emotion; a fine link surely connects his world to the adult world, like Ariadne's thread.

In that Greek myth, Theseus introduces himself into the labyrinth at Knossos to confront the dangerous Minotaur. In order to find his way back to the entrance gallery, he unrolls behind him a reel of thread which Ariadne has given him; he prevails over the Minotaur and goes back to the source of the thread, thus making his act meaningful.

From this point of view, the year 1974 was of special importance to me; it was one of those turning points in one's life, a piece of Ariadne's thread. I was barely sixteen, living nostalgically in Lausanne in the remembrance of my Apollo days, thinking that the most beautiful part of my life had already gone. I can see myself again at the window of a tea-room, noticing for the first time a kind of rigid parachute gliding over the Alps, keeping my eyes wide open to work out what it was. Then came the rush to the landing site and the first questions. It's called a hang glider, it weighs about thirty pounds and it allows you to glide for a few minutes, starting off from a mountainous slope. It was the very beginning of that new sport and three passionate youths had come to this Alpine resort in order to promote it under the leadership of the pioneer Etienne Rithner. For me, it was love at first sight! I had thought that aviation had made it possible to explore everything, including the Moon, that there was no more room for inventions, and suddenly I realised that back in the Apollo days the simplest flying machine didn't exist. And its simplicity is precisely what makes it interesting, because it doesn't rely on technique but on sensitivity and intuition. The spectacular aspect of it isn't an outer journey some 180,000 miles away from the Earth, but the intimate experience of a short-lived flight. This time, man is at the forefront again, not the machine.

Up until then, I had always been quite fearful, even though the idea of facing a risk fascinated me. When I was ten, King Baudoin of Belgium had asked me what I would like to be and I'd said:

"A stuntman, your Majesty!"

In fact, my only attempt at overcoming vertigo was prematurely brought to a halt because of a knot that had formed itself while I was roping down from our balcony. After being stuck in the air for a very long time, and being brought down by my relatives who'd heard me shout, I gave up on doing stunts. But when I saw, in the grass, that rudimentary hang glider which had allowed its pilot to glide from the top of the Meilleret, suddenly it was like an immense challenge. Why not me? A few weeks before, I had reached the minimum age required but I still needed permission from my parents. My mother always had great faith in life but my father usually felt happier if he could rely on good calculations. For the first hang gliders, there were no calculations but a few tubes cut with a hand saw, some holes bored with a drill and a sail cut with scissors. Yet, after a few days of intensive family negotiations, passion prevailed over technique and I was learning to fly.

I cannot describe the first impression of the harness becoming taught, my feet leaving the ground and the wing bending under the effect of my bodily movements. For indeed, it was my body that made the hang glider turn, not my head or mental ability. A feeling of lightness but also a sense of wholeness surrounded me for several days after this first ground hop.

Following these initial five metres, there were longer flights, each one more fabulous than the previous one: by night, in a two-seater, at high altitude, launched from hot-air balloons, motorised, with acrobatics… I established a new relationship with nature, with birds, but especially with myself. The accidents I suffered, the dramatic deaths of several friends, the moments of doubt or questioning which I went through, were all vital experiences that also shaped the course of my life.

But I wasn't aware of it yet, and, spellbound by my discoveries and my new adventures, I wanted to keep following a trace in the sky. In fact, I agreed wholeheartedly with Kierkegaard: "It is better to lose, out of passion, than to lose passion".

The ecstasy of my first big flight in a hang glider died down abruptly as I crashed on the roof of a chalet, and I know I was very lucky to get away with it so lightly that day.

It was a very striking experience, yet, from all my rough notes it seems I don't really know how to talk about it. No matter how much I search inside me, I cannot put the words together. A bad estimation of the altitude, too slow a turn on the downwind leg and a head-on crash with a chimney. In an instant, I knew the flight was going to end that way; I was certain that it couldn't be otherwise, that all I had gone through so far could only converge to make me live this experience, this overwhelming impression that my life formed part of a logical path, that it followed the course of Things.

Inexorability is almost acceptable when you can see through it, when it seems to be part of a scheme. Ordeals only make sense if you understand, if only be for a fraction of a second, that they are meant to teach you, to leave some landmarks in your life; and that it is up to us to find their meaning, instead of complaining. It was clear that this flight would change many things for me and that I would never be the same again. This accident left me feeling fatalistic for a long time; I kept on thinking of all the circum stances, starting from the very idea of spending my holidays in the mountains, that had led me to finish them in hospital. So many elements had been linked and combined for me to crash precisely on that chalet – not against the power line five yards away to the right, nor in the cosy meadow situated a bit further on – and for a rabbit hutch to be there to cushion my fall.

My entire family was present that day, and, naturally, everyone encouraged me to give up on my emancipation in the air! But all I had in mind were the images of my flight. I could recall with such precision my preparation for the takeoff and the instructor saying in a calm voice:

'OK, you can go when you want!'

I could still feel the trapeze which I had held to balance the wing, and the strength – new to me – which had made me take the necessary steps to jump into emptiness. Up until then, I had suffered vertigo when climbing a tree and my clumsiness used to make my PE teacher laugh at school; but now I knew there existed a state of being, of lucidity, which could make you surpass yourself totally. I had no idea what it was, but I realised that the topics of my first philosophical readings weren't mere abstract theories, that they truly described inner experiences, to be lived in practical terms: I'd had the opportunity to discover for myself, in an instant, that the most fascinating part of our lives couldn't be perceived from an ordinary stance and that, in fact, we were part of a much bigger whole that might give sense to incomprehensible things. But at the time, the only tool I had to explore the invisible was a rudimentary wing.

Therefore, there was no question of my giving up on flying. On the contrary, I wanted to make use of my teenage passion to go even further, to understand other things, to solve mysteries while experiencing the strongest of sensations. I wanted to go beyond human and technical limits, to know fear and audacity, to increase my freedom. Little by little flying became a necessity. Weather forecasts became my major weekly preoccupation, and, on more than one occasion, I flew through thick layers of fog, under rain, under snow, so as not to lose a single day of hang gliding. I needed to exist within Nature and in my case this communion brought me enough energy to bear life as a schoolboy. I was getting dependent on this new feeling to such an extent that, on several occasions, I convinced my mother to come and fetch me from school with my wing loaded on top of the car, ready to go and make the last flight of the day, facing the sunset over Lake Geneva. It all seemed so simple; all I needed was to make a few steps in the direction of the wind in order to leave all preoccupations behind, to abandon all problems and worries and, while gliding silently in another world, find the motivation that made me live from one week-end to another.

Then a friend of mine was killed, and I went through a period of great doubts. I had helped him to take off with his Quicksilver only a few minutes before he crashed against a rock face. His death shocked me so much that, during several months spent without flying, I tried to understand it over and over again. It was in this questioning mood, free of any rational reasoning, that I started to look for the answer through a wide variety of fields. It was my first contact with astrology, but also with I Ching. It was also the first time that my dreams provided me with precise explanations. Through the study of the planets and of Chinese sticks (two sciences based on five thousand years of symbolic tradition), the signs of Life were apparent; or, rather, my temporary open-mindedness enabled me to perceive them. Our existence is sprinkled with these signs, the testimony of a higher world which we neglect because we cannot explain it rationally.

Unable to publicly express such intimate emotions, I embarked with a childhood friend on the making of an amateur film which we called 'Hang gliding from the first to the seventh heaven'. Three kilometres of rush and a script that changed as often as our thoughts and was never completed. escaping the ghetto of a dull and boring daily life and wanting to stretch himself to his limits, our 'hero' started practising several extreme sports in a race forward that made him gradually dependent, addicted to his artificial paradise, before his intuition finally told him that a mystical quest through escapism could only lead to other drugs, which would be a dead end.

Not yet familiar with Gurdjieff's thinking or with Chinese cosmology, I was beginning to feel that the path I had followed was a dangerous one, but I didn't know any other. My ignorance and the naivety proper to an eighteen-year old let me down before the end of the story. I lacked the vocabulary to speak about psychological or spiritual evolution or the development of Consciousness. I didn't even know what that was about. I was also totally ignorant of the fact that the moments you want to avoid are precisely those that contain the main keys to the answers. In this aspect, my book may be a new version of that aborted film attempt, since I am still following a trace in the sky in order to get a better understanding of life on earth.

In any case, at that time I started to prefer to Kierkegaard the dialogue between Jonathan Livingston and Maureen in a film inspired by Richard Bach's book:

"Can I really learn to fly without limits?"

"You may discover something that's even more important to you than flying without limits. You will learn what perfection really is. In the meantime, let's first try and learn to fly properly".

There are so many traps, so many mirages and illusions in our existence that I could only but feel the whole weight of the term 'really'.

At an age when my friends were becoming specialists in disco-theques, the striking events I was living gave me an inkling that life as such has a meaning and that maybe man's purpose is to discover it; that we only use up a tenth or a hundredth of our capacity of understanding because we ignore the importance of what our nor-mal senses cannot perceive. At that time, our philosophy teacher was telling us about Plato and we were discovering the Myth of the Cave. Being school children, we would learn it from memory, we would recite it in its every detail, intellectualising it, as if it wasn't obvious or clear enough, as if it didn't follow naturally.

I could sum it up here in a few words: our every day world is compared to a cave with a large opening, and humans are like prisoners with chains that prevent them from seeing anything else but the rock opposite the entrance. Their only occupation, therefore, consists in watching on that wall the animated two-dimensional shadows coming from the beings that live outside in broad daylight, commenting on them and judging them. Their vision is the only real perception they have of the world, since this is all they have known throughout their lives. If one of them was suddenly freed and taken outside the cave, he would be blinded by the light and wouldn't be able to see anything at first. That would make him miss the world he had always known. But, gradually, he would get used to a three-dimensional existence under the light and would not want to go back to his cave; in any case, his eyes being accustomed to daylight, he would no longer be able to distinguish shadows; and the other prisoners, having decided that he was mad, would definitely not want to abandon their own way of living. And Plato adds:

"The eyes may be troubled in two ways and for two opposite reasons: turning from light to darkness, and turning from darkness to light".

I felt all this intensely. That description of the world, with its two levels, a lower and a higher one, had become instinctively familiar to me and this myth was only putting some words to a concept I had already understood. But I still didn't know much about going from one level to the other. It now seemed clear that sudden exposure to light with untrained eyes could explain, in part, my first accident and those a few other friends had suffered. Besides, I began to understand why some drug addicts don't want to 'come down' after some very intense visions; and I began to feel drawn by those we call 'mad', by beings who fight the horror of living in the Cave through delirium and hallucinations. For Plato:

"A man who perceives beauty on Earth remembers true Beauty again; his Soul acquires wings; it becomes eager to fly and reach the heights. Feeling unable to do so, it looks up towards the sky, like a bird; and, neglecting to care for earthly things, it is accused of madness, but the rapture which elevates it is the most beautiful of deliriums…"

I remember a few particularly intense flights which plunged me into a trance for several days afterwards, with a sense of happiness and plenitude. It was a stimulating state, it gave my life a meaning, but it also left me on the edge. I no longer had the same preoccupations as my schoolmates, and I still hadn't found a group to share my investigations with. In fact, the only person I could discuss these topics with was my mother. For hours on end, we shared our experiences and thoughts about life, comparing our readings or the currents of thoughts we'd come across, to build up some theories on the meaning of things. From my early childhood I had been going on long walks with her in the countryside; during these, beyond all the words exchanged, I could feel the presence of a sweet light of harmony inside me. I can recall very clearly the first sensation of being consciously living the moment to the full.

Later, I would still have an intense liking for what seemed so natural to me as a child, because my mother had showed me how to preserve the vital lead. Being the daughter of a protestant preacher herself, she'd had the tolerance and open-mindedness to let me pursue a path away from any dogmatic approach, allowing me to develop what every child brings with him when he comes to the world.

Wernher von Braun's autograph was coming back to me:

'To Bertrand Piccard, who, I hope, will continue the Piccard family tradition of exploring both inner and outer space'.

The words 'inner space' were beginning to take on a special meaning. My quest for the supreme flight had progressively increased my marked interest in the 'inner space'. I now wished to go deeper into that theme from the psychological point of view, so, why not study medicine and psychiatry? That could be a means of reconciling my passion for flying with a profession. The fundamental advantage of psychiatry was, as I saw it, that it would allow me to go deeper into my research while studying the situation of those who dared to question their existence too. In other words, to reflect with patients on the means of acquiring a more global vision of life. It wasn't so much a question of studying what made people ill, as of understanding what inner resources we must develop to be more fulfilled.

Before I started studying at university, people would often ask me whether I was going to be 'like dad' and 'like granddad', inferring the difficulty involved in bearing that name and in feeling obliged to continue with a tradition of scientific research and invention. Every time I developed a passionate interest in something during my childhood, my dreams and the utopia that things would be easy prevented me from perceiving the true implication of these questions. During my 'Cape Kennedy' period, I could see myself become an astronaut in the NASA. Later, while studying Antiquity, I felt sure that I could discover Atlantis if I became an archaeologist. It was equally obvious to me that I would eventually create a revolutionary diving suit, in order to go hand in hand with my father to the bottom of the 37,000 ft deep Mariana Trench!

It was easy to represent the 'third generation' when you had a whole life ahead of you, rubbing shoulders with extraordinary people who were so indulgent with a teenager who hadn't proved anything yet. One day, at a reception, a minister had called me 'the Swiss hope' and the head of the Greek government, learning of the passion I then had for archaeology, had even placed a helicopter at our disposal to visit the Santorini excavation; I was fourteen, and my first sight of Cape Sunion, while flying above the Aegean sea at sunset, was one of the most exciting moments of my 'golden childhood'.

I still thought I could do it all. I wasn't yet torn between the glory of perpetuating the family tradition and the desire to draw nearer to the meaning of Life. That dilemma would come later. The conversations of a spiritual nature which livened up the long walks with my mother had nurtured my inborn need to understand human Beings. But I thought it was easy to reconcile everything, outer and inner investigations, fame and meditation, the flashes of cameras and those of consciousness!

I didn't feel the need to find my way in life, following a trace, on earth, under water or in the sky. Not until I was old enough to go to university. I remember that deciding not to 'be like dad', not to become an engineer or a physicist, but a doctor, was a very difficult decision to reach. It was probably the first choice I ever made consciously, and I remember it with stunning precision. Allowed to follow my intuition even if that meant abandoning the family tradition, I was not manipulated by my close relatives, who had perhaps already sensed the relevance of that sentence by Richard Bach:

"You are not the child of the people you call mother and father, but their fellow-adventurer on a bright journey to understand the things that are".

I'd had a foretaste, an instinctive feeling of these 'things that are' during the most intense moments of my flights, those instants which had given me an intimate sense of wholeness, of eternity. I wanted to continue exploring it, and make this investigation my profession. So, I started studying medicine.

In fact, I followed a route full of zigzags, sometimes marked with stops and starts. I left university for three years in order to set up Piccard Aviation, a microlight company; I engaged in a political and juridical battle in favour of ultra-light flying, forbidden in Switzerland; then there were a few record competitions and 'firsts' to draw media attention, but, every time, I found myself caught up with 'inner space', with what directs life to give it sense, inside you. This is why, when I realised that my company wasn't having the commercial success I'd hoped for, I decided to finish my studies, stronger from… my experience.

Looking back on the ground covered since the Cape Kennedy days, this verse from a Leonard Cohen song seems to have been written for me:

'It's like our visit to the moon or to that other star: I guess you go for nothing if you really want to go that far'.

Aeronautics, which had filled my eyes with wonder through its conquest of the stars when I was a child, eventually brought me back to something much closer but equally unknown: Life in general and human Beings in particular. Far away from the stratosphere, from the Pacific ocean trenches and from Cape Kennedy, but perhaps thanks to them… and to Ariadne's thread.

Between Icarus
and Daedalus

There is a third way

My Books on anatomy were neatly kept in the briefcase that lay deep inside my car. Missing my lectures at university was a weight off my shoulders. An hour earlier, I had taken off from a snowy peak to make the most of the first spring thermals. Next to me, what I had first taken to be a sparrow hawk started spiralling upwards under a storm cloud. Since it was showing me the way, I decided to approach it. But the closer I got, the further away it seemed. This was no small bird of prey by my side, it was an enormous beast hundreds of yards away. In fact, it was an eagle. Knowing how crucial it was to remain below him to avoid being attacked, I directed my hang glider in the same upward direction and went a few hundred yards up with him before going my own way. I travelled from peak to peak, from cloud to cloud, relying only on the strength of rising currents of air.

Now, would anyone believe me if I said I was actually preparing myself for an exam in medicine? Yet, that's exactly what I was doing! I needed to delve into my power of concentration and distance myself from my lectures, to place my exams back into the context of what I was seeking. And also, to refocus on the essence of contacts with Nature and with myself, to recharge my batteries and, after landing, live my student life more efficiently.

My first years of hang gliding had shown me the extent to which coping with dangerous situations during a flight could help me to deal with daily stressful situations. I had learned to feel at ease with unforeseen events and the risks inherent in life. My power of concentration and quick reactions had already got me out of serious trouble on many occasions. Panicking is often more disastrous than danger itself and I had learned to avoid it at all costs. Admittedly, to reach that goal, I had sometimes gone through the school of fright! Especially during my first launch with a hang glider from a hot-air balloon.

That day, I was so delighted at the thought of making my entry into the world of aeronauts at Château-d'Œx, that I shared my feelings with one of them. He said:

"As I understand it, you're going to be stupidly hanging from the end of a cable before starting a perfectly normal flight!"

Before laughing at his remark, I had to wait until I was 'stupidly hanging' in the Alps 10,000 ft above ground, with a hang glider shaking so much that the gondola was in danger of spewing its pilot out. I had to wait until I had achieved some fabulous flights, gliding through a sky full of hot-air balloons at Château d'Œx, like a butterfly going from flower to flower. Then I knew that these launches give you sensations which you do not experience with a 'normal flight'.

There is a beginning to everything. During my first attempt, both the aeronaut and I accumulated a series of mistakes. The cable connecting the hang glider to the balloon was too long. The release could only be operated from the gondola and the speed of descent we had fixed was excessive for a launch. Right from the start, the hang glider began to act as an aerofoil and revolved faster and faster round the axis of the ropes. Before the aeronaut could operate the release, the hang glider was circling round the balloon, getting all the ropes mixed up and winding them round the wicker basket. There was a sudden crash, then total silence. I thought the pilot had managed to launch me. In fact, it was only the ropes which had slid under a corner of the gondola, giving a bit more slack. Just as the hang glider dropped down, the ropes suddenly tautened again, pulling it higher up than the gondola, like a dog on a leash. At this stage, pushed back by the ropes of the basket, it toppled over and was dragged down violently by the falling balloon. The movement was progressively accentuated to the point of inclining the balloon at 45° with the basket on its side. Meanwhile, the aeronaut was keeping busy. Clinging to the frame to avoid being ejected, he had to wait for the basket to pass under the envelope every time, to fire the burners without setting the balloon on fire. No need to tell you that in such circumstances cutting the cable to free me was out of the question. It is difficult to tell how long it was before the fall – which had probably reached 33 ft per second – was finally cushioned and I stopped swaying. We managed to go back up to 10,000 ft, unravel the ropes and do a proper launch.

That day I was really frightened, but it never crossed my mind that I could be killed. The hardest thing was being totally dependent on the pilot of the hot-air balloon, I had no means of freeing myself. I had taken the risk of crashing without being the direct cause of my accident. This experience strengthened my need to be always in full control of myself and of my acts. Admittedly, this is something we are not used to in our daily life. A great number of laws, regulations and other guarantees tend to spare citizens from having to think. Our overprotective society, bent on supervising and reassuring its members as a whole, inevitably smothers them individually. The rules which safeguard the community can only exist to the detriment of one's own responsibility. Safe from the main dangers of existence, we live longer and longer, more and more protected and reassured, without learning to evaluate our own share of responsibility in our life. As a natural consequence, we become dependent on all that guarantees our artificial safety. We learn to follow a pattern without thinking or investigating. We start reproducing faithfully what we've learned, reacting to life like a well-programmed computer, without developing new behaviours, without creating or innovating. In this pattern of presumed safety, when a piece of the puzzle is missing, the whole thing falls apart. You only need to see the chaos at a crossroads when the traffic lights break down. You then realise to what extent we've lost the habit of thinking for ourselves, to what extent we rely on force of habit. When a problem arises, we reassure ourselves thinking it wasn't our fault, convinced that life is cruel after all. But in fact, we are simply not ready, we haven't yet developed the means to evolve in life. In future, if I had an accident, at least I wanted to be the cause of it.

That first experience at the 'school of fright' had another consequence: I had no stage fright when completing my medical exam papers a few weeks later. On the contrary, I felt quite detached, yet it was the most decisive exam in my medical studies! At least, everything was of minor importance in comparison with what I had just gone through.

I began to realise that all those activities reminding us that we are responsible for the course of our own life can bring us a breath of fresh air on a personal level. The appearance, not to say outburst, in the seventies and eighties of so-called high-risk sports may have been a reaction against citizens being turned into robots. The word 'vigilance' takes on a new meaning when your life is in your hands, whether through a trapeze, the opening-system of a parachute, or a rock to be climbed bare-handed. Your own existence takes on a new dimension, it acquires a special flavour when you learn to preserve it personally, when you are in charge of it.

It was probably thanks to this gift of vigilance that I survived my first loop with the hang glider. You cannot be taught aerobatics, you can only rely on your intuition and on direct knowledge. A figure can be correct or incorrect and yet the difference is very slim. The only way to try was to get on with it.

And here I was, launching from a superb multicoloured hot-air balloon, increasing my speed and veering to the right: I managed a great 'wing over'. There was a second speed increase, and an overturn shifting to the left. I thought I was ready for the loop but I hadn't held my speed long enough before the final push. The hang glider nosed right up and I lost sight of the earth, ascending vertically towards the blue, blue sky. Then I noticed a decrease in the speed and all came to a standstill: not a sound around me, I was floating. The world was topsy-turvy and so was my heart. The hang glider remained in a static position on its back and I fell on the sail. I clung to the trapeze instinctively and ended up STANDING on my hang glider. It all happened so slowly, it was like landing on top of a cloud, even though the situation was critical as far as aerodynamics were concerned. After several fruitless attempts at turning the right way round, I moved a leg backwards towards the nose of the hang glider and kicked it heavily while opening an aileron. This provoked a dive followed by half a barrel roll and I was back to a normal flying position, totally entangled in my harness. I had lost 1300 feet and my reputation as a cautious pilot all in one go. But I had done my first loop, that mythical figure in aviation where, for a moment, it isn't the Earth that goes round but man.

The displays, done as an amateur so far, became more and more numerous. For my stunt flying, I first combined a hang glider with a hot-air balloon, then with a parachute. These were the days of the 'air trio': drop in a two-seater hang glider (improved technique!), from which, in turn, a parachutist would make a jump. We liked this manoeuvre because it allowed us to show three different types of air sports. We would take off together… before a spectacular severing of the umbilical cord, each of us then carrying on with the flight in his own way. Then the media coverage added to the pleasure of flying. Since this was a world first among the small circle of adventurers (back in 1982), pictures of these events were widely broadcast. This propelled me into the world of air shows. Nevertheless, I found the 'circus' aspect of the air trio a little embarrassing. It seemed to me that aerobatics made people dream a lot more. After the display of the national patrols and their jet engines, I would show with great satisfaction a full programme of spins, loops and wingovers in a non-motorised ultralight. I felt I was sharing with the audience something more accessible, more tangible. With merely a canvas and some tubes a man was able to 'explore happiness in three dimensions', to quote Bernard Chabbert, the famous air show commentator. When I punctuated my displays with smoke and put the music from Jonathan Livingston in the background, especially the piece called 'Be', I could sometimes see arabesques in the eyes of the spectators who came and spoke to me afterwards. On occasions, the impact was deeper and a few smiles exchanged were enough to have the certainty we were following the same trace.

Because of all the opportunities that came my way to do a display, and the media coverage that ensued, many pilots in my club must have felt jealous of me at times. Yet, I very often provoked my own luck. For a long time, I believed in predestination. In the end, I reckon that what we are predestined for is not the experiences we go through but the choices we are faced with. If we are not really responsible for the events that occur, we are certainly responsible for the way we face them. In most cases, we are free to say yes or no to the possibilities we are given. I don't think life is predetermined, but that doesn't mean it unfolds at random; in this sense, it is a dichotomy: it divides and subdivides itself in groups of two continuously, like successive branching. Destiny would then be like a vast network on which man makes a move by accepting or refusing the choices offered to him.

I remember the first time I saw a hot-air balloon fly. I could have stayed at home, but I followed it. After watching it land, I could have gone home like the other onlookers, but I went to ask the pilot how he felt about dropping a hang glider. Two months later, he called me back and invited me to the first hot-air balloon display in Château d'Œx. I have already related what followed.

I took part in many air shows. They are exceptional meeting places. Every year throughout the world, they bring together several million people who have come to see for themselves a dream that may well be accessible to them. They feel that perhaps they could try it too, that pilots are not so much heroes but enthusiasts... or investigators. I came across test pilots and astronauts who were still able to marvel at the perfection of an aircraft in flight, but also some ordinary city dwellers who had broken their piggy bank to treat themselves to a first flight: they set foot on our planet again with glittering eyes, thanking the sky for the invitation.

I myself cannot believe I waited for so long before doing my first free fall. For the price of a good meal, I had fed on a new sensation, that of being in physical contact with the sky which had swallowed me, feeling drowned in vastness and being part of it. I had just jumped from a Dakota 14,000 ft above the ground, in tandem with an instructor. He spent his life making beginners discover his world, thanks to a two-seater harness. I must confess that I learned more about life in sixty seconds than in several months. Anyone can experience the same, provide they believe their existence deserves a third or a fourth dimension ...

This spurred me to learn to use a parachute to be able to jump from the plane without being ejected by an instructor. Apart from the extraordinary sensation procured by flying without a hang glider, resting on air with my arms and legs, the most fascinating moment had been coming out of the plane. Crouching still before the open door, ready to jump in a deafening abyss, I recognised the very symbol of life, a mixture of fear and trust which marks every action or decision. On one side, there was the voice of safety, of 'reason', of stillness, advising me to give up, to refuse to go on this stupid and useless adventure, introducing doubt and fear in my attempt at exploring new horizons. On the other, there was the voice of trust in life, movement, evolution, taking on responsibilities and risks. Both voices got mixed up and buzzed in my head, fighting over my decision. I was both held back and pushed forward. Feeling totally paralysed, I was fascinated by what was going on inside me and waited to see which voice would dominate. Each time, it was the voice of trust and I was propelled into the sky with arms open, without having to decide.

Hang gliding and free fall skydiving don't have the monopoly of the so-called high-risk sports. A great number of other activities are here to prove that our society needs to be in direct touch again with the environment, but also that people need to be in touch with themselves, their sensations, their emotions. The new sports allow you to go beyond barren rationalism and experience fully what it means to be human : paragliding, microlighting, mountain-biking, roller-blades, snowboards, bare-foot, climbing with bare-hands, apnea diving, bunji jumping, hydrospeed, etc. If you think about it, there is nothing contradictory about the fact that it is precisely in this era of space technology that some sportsmen and women try to return to their own essence by throwing themselves from a bridge with their feet attached to a fifty-five yard elastic band! Since our society no longer offers the means to transcend its technical and materialistic façade, a certain number of people will inevitably seek elsewhere a bit of responsibility, some fragments of a more global truth.

These modern sports are also different because of their spectacular aspect and the identification process offered to the public: you 'experience' extreme adventures sitting in front of your television, and you wear fluorescent sportswear to have the appearance of a professional. But, in fact, it is the inner part of the experience which is fluorescent.

The way is now open to test your own limits rather than those of a machine. You use your body like an engine or a steering mechanism, your sensitiveness and intuition prime over your mental capacity. In short, this allows you to discover an inner and unknown 'dimension' which the requirements of daily life would not let you see. This 'dimension' consists in feeling that you exist within the action but also within yourself; you are open to what surrounds you, but also to yourself. You are 'simply' present, you are truly here and now.

When I learned to fly, this encounter with the present moment moved me deeply. I had suddenly discovered something no one had ever taught me before, either at school or elsewhere.

Up until then, I had been taught the importance of the past, as the source of experience and traditions, the origin of knowledge. We had to know the past to understand ourselves. All of which is true, but not sufficient.

Of course, I had also been taught the importance of the future, in which we must learn to project ourselves, which we have to plan methodically to make sure all future existence is balanced. Yet, scientific investigation had shown that ninety per cent of life events happen in a completely unforeseeable and haphazard manner. So, is it worth devoting all our time to the planning of the remaining ten per cent? The future is important, indeed, but does it have to justify all our efforts? If you think about it, the only time when we can change something in our life is neither in the past nor in the future but in the present, at this very instant.

Before that, we are already in the past, it's too late; as to the future, it sounds like 'maybe', we haven't got to it yet. Nevertheless, the human mind is forever obsessed with parasitic thoughts, about what we should have done before and what we could do later. These thoughts are often pointless, they play no part in our life apart from absorbing a good deal of energy. What I had discovered in the hang glider was that facing danger had obliged me to refocus on the present. This was even more perceptible with aerobatic flights.

To loop the loop, a pilot has no other tool but his sensitivity. He has to gauge the speed of his hang glider through every quivering of the sail, every hissing of the cables, through the impact of the wind on his face. Then he has to choose the right fraction of a second to push the trapeze away, softly, then more strongly, before pulling it back to complete the loop and pass on to the next figure. If the traction is too long the speed increases dangerously, which could break the structure. If it's too short, the hang glider will not gain enough speed and will get stuck on its back before tumbling forward. This is why you need to see and feel everything at the same time, to do everything at the right moment. The amount of data you have to process simultaneously is enormous. There is always a risk of getting overwhelmed and losing control.

But what fascinated me with every loop and every spin, was to observe how self-awareness throughout enabled me to deal with all these impressions at the same time. The centre of gravity of my priorities would suddenly shift and propel me to the very present: the concentration needed in order to rectify the perilous situation allowed no time for daily worries, and even showed me, sometimes, how trivial these were. There was no room for the past or the future, for the association of ideas that cluttered my brain, the fancies that monopolised my emotions, or the automatic reflexes that often directed my life.

I could not agree with Descartes's famous statement "I think therefore I am". It was obvious to me that you cannot be while you are thinking. While you are thinking, you lose yourself in the past or in the future, you disperse into other times and other places, and therefore you cannot exist in the present. For me, the only way to 'be' was to feel all the impressions of the moment and to stop time through a new formula:

"I feel, therefore I am".

That experience confirmed that studying psychiatry, and above all psychotherapy, had been the right choice. There was no question of inciting patients to engage in high-risk activities, of course. But there had to be some way of exploiting life's hardest moments to teach them how to make use of their inner resources by developing their self-consciousness. This way, they would have a greater control over their evolution.

When recording some aerobatic sessions with Nicolas Hulot's team, on the ground, I had many reasons for being full of ideas of all kinds. Then, some cameras were fixed at the tips of the hang glider, with heavy counterweights, a video recorder was attached to my back and a microphone was placed near my mouth, all this to show 'what I was capable of' in one of the most popular TV programmes of the time: Ushuaïa. Nevertheless, once in the air, magic took hold of me again: there was no room for anything else but the air blowing in the sail, the pressure of the trapeze against my fingers, and this incredible sight of the earth bustling below while I felt so calm and serene. When I moved on to a spin after looping the loop, I didn't even think that several million spectators were going to see that move. I had left my pride down below. The worries I may have had when taking off, whether to do with my family, finances or profession, suddenly didn't matter anymore. In fact, my own personality, my usual way of responding to life, didn't matter either, since I was precisely doing something totally unusual.

Alone with myself, in a kind of relaxed concentration and action, experiencing a sensation of my body through movement, I was slowly able to witness the development of an intuitive sense of the Essence, of another form of self-consciousness. Not only was i alive, but I could feel I was.

If this consciousness proves to be insufficient for one reason or another (unhealthy diet, tiredness, an excess of impressions received compared to the amount you can deal with), indigestion and panic will follow. Vertigo is an eloquent example, quite similar to homesickness. Indeed, what are vertigo or homesickness if not a projection of oneself, along a vertical or horizontal axis, to a place other than where we live at the time? And projection necessarily means dispersion, therefore an insufficient consciousness of oneself. Those who have suffered vertigo know what it's like to want to leave the air and be on the firm ground again. This wish can turn into an obsession. Some people are in such a hurry to get back down that they jump into emptiness! This is known as the mysterious call of emptiness ... yet there is no more mystery about it than a tree with shallow roots being blown down by the wind.

Some exercises consisting in reminding yourself that you are here, that you are presently within the situation and within yourself, can give spectacular refocusing results. Based on the modification of the breathing pattern, amongst other things, they can even cure your sensation of vertigo or fear. I have to specify that these exercises are so natural to some people that they are probably not aware of them, while for others, these are so far removed from their lifestyle that they can't even imagine their existence. All this may explain individual tolerance to danger, or the tendency to seek strong impressions.

On the contrary, it would be ridiculous to believe that seeking danger is the only way to feel our presence, to develop self-consciousness. There are many other less artificial means, such as music, dance, art or meditation, but that would give us enough material for another book. In fact, much has been written on that theme.

One thing was at least clear to me: living an ordinary life, without seeking or surpassing your self, borders on hypoglycaemia or mindlessness – either through lack of impressions or through the inability to subtly catch those we are presented with.

It is fascinating to develop a taste for this new sensation – a mixture of wholeness and responsibility, a sensation often discovered by chance and which you cannot always explain. Then there is a risk of being seduced by achievement, record-breaking, like some inaccessible goal which you can only reach through strong will or courage. It's a mad, intoxicating run: you want to go higher up, further away, lower down, to get near the limits of the possible; and sometimes beyond … The myth of Icarus is here to remind us of the danger. Ignoring the warnings proffered by his father Daedalus, Icarus got seduced by the freedom his flight gave him and got too close to the sun. The heat melted the wax that held his feathers and he made a deadly fall.

Craving for strong impressions can make us addicted to our passion, as if it were a drug. It doesn't matter if the weather forecast is bad, if we lack the necessary training or if our equipment is not adequate, provided we can thrive again on that extraordinary sensation, which itself becomes a source of intoxication, a drug! But, while drugs allow us to forget daily vicissitudes momentarily by making us believe in an artificial paradise, they also make us forget our self. There is no room left for self-consciousness, and sometimes no room for reflection, or the survival instinct. Then disaster occurs. The sorcerer's apprentice becomes a victim of his own badly mastered power. Some call it endogenous addiction because, in such extreme conditions, the body starts producing stress hormones like adrenaline but also endorphins, a kind of physiological morphine. The discharge of these substances into the blood stream during a violent stimulus would explain the organic origin of the intoxication. The more you wait to pull the parachute, the longer the elastic, the stronger the wind, the greater the 'high'.

The need some people have to constantly face danger and stretch their limits can also be explained from a psychological approach. I am referring to the different personality patterns, in other words, the set of mechanisms used by individuals from early childhood to adapt to their environment. Briefly speaking, a harmoniously developed personality is that which has found the right balance between thought and action on one hand, and between inner subjectivity and external reality on the other. Therefore, a constant need for action or for testing one's limits expresses an unconscious attempt at resolving, outside oneself, some unbearable inner tension or controlling 'vital anguish' (depression). Without going into details, I shall limit myself to a few examples.

Those who haven't had a proper opportunity to learn how to use thoughts and communication in order to deal with their emotions and feelings, normally give priority to action in their life. Those who haven't managed to assimilate, to interiorise figures of authority, what we call the superego in Freudian terms, are obliged to actively confront external rules and limits in order to feel reassured and function properly; they defy social laws and sometimes natural laws, such as gravitation, equilibrium, meteorology or human psychology. They have to confront reality to find their right place and feel psychologically complete.

Other types of people need more than a challenge to feel alive, they have to triumph over risk and danger. They unconsciously try to improve their self-esteem through victories over the environment. Such gratification makes their poor self-esteem more bearable to them. The delight in controlling a surplus of affects, which may go as far as a complete denial of limits, can lead to a feeling of omnipotence as can be observed in suicidal behaviour: skiing down breathtaking icy rock faces, taking off in a paraglider during a storm, etc.

I remember a particularly turbulent flight in a paraglider which forced me to land prematurely in order to save my skin. Another pilot held the flight for an hour and declared afterwards:

"It was fabulous, my sail folded up with every turbulence, I nearly got killed at least ten times. What a great flight!"

At this stage, the anthropologist David Le Breton would talk of ordeal. That ancient ritual, now trivialised by some high-risk sports, consists in confronting death to prove to yourself that life has a meaning.

Psychologists and psychiatrists too often stop the analysis at this stage. They only consider human beings in relation to their personality, leaving aside their deeper inner values. The problem often lies in the fact that scientists study their subjects from the outside. Therefore, they can only observe their superficial aspects. My flights in a hang glider, and what I discovered through them, made me feel like plunging to the very core of the situations, at the very heart of experiences, to become both the observer and the subject of the study. Without disowning my scientific background, I started using aviation as a laboratory to study the inner world. My grandfather had used it to explore the outer world.

It was thus striking to see how these extreme sports, and the act of confronting the risks they implied, can be an aim as much as a means. An aim, because, as psychological theories demonstrate, they may be practised unconsciously to improve the structure of a fragile or fragmented personality, to get a kick out of adrenaline or strong impressions, to shine through an unusual activity or to escape from a boring life. And a means, because, by disclosing other important values inherent to human beings, by 'getting to see' beyond personality, they provide new scopes to those who are open to it. In other words, an aim or a means, depending on one's state of mind, on the interest or meaning you give to your life, on what you try to 'do' … or 'be'.

Although my daily life was not revolutionised overnight, I was beginning to perceive how a more intimate relationship with your self, with your sensitivities and your intuition, allowed for a certain transformation in life, especially in your relationship with others. Having been able to step back, your vision of life can only be modified towards a greater comprehension, and greater humility. You cannot be quite the same ever again once you have discovered that there is something else, and that this something else lies inside you.

After my first experiences with a hang glider, a friend of my mother's, who led personal development therapy groups, told me that the feeling of consciousness I described when talking to her about my flights was, in fact, the very state one reaches through a spiritual quest. In her opinion, a few meditation exercises would allow me to drop my aeronautical 'crutches'. I saw later that she was right. Nevertheless, if my hang gliding adventures had not provided me with all the answers, they had at least given me a foretaste and the wish to find them.

My family background could have prompted me to develop ultralight flying from a technological or aerodynamic point of view. On the other hand, I could have chosen the way of intoxication and fascination which this type of sport can cause, and lose myself in the process. Yet, it seemed to me that half way between Daedalus, the scientific inventor, and Icarus, the euphoric adventurer, there must have be a third way. It was in this direction that I was pushed while following a trace in the sky. This book is here to tell you more about it.

ARABESQUES

Straight lines don't take you to heaven

THE TAKEOFF WAS FROM MONT-GROS, 2300 ft above Monaco harbour, at 11 a.m. on 4th October 1986. Spectators and pilots were gathered. The former, impatiently waiting for the event, the latter preparing their hang gliders in silence, concentrating hard on the first round of the Ilinx, 'feel the whirling, feel the vertigo', European aerobatic hang gliding championship. There was a velvety atmosphere, difficult to describe. An atmosphere proper to high level competitions. And the Ilinx was one of them.

The competitors had finished assembling their aircraft and some of them were rehearsing their programmes, with their eyes shut, sitting cross-legged or steering an invisible bar between their hands. Doing acrobatics in a hang glider was no longer a novelty, but it was still like a wild beast to be approached cautiously, to be tamed and gently brought under control. It showed off everyone's personality, their quiet or aggressive side, without room for deceit; it was a competition against oneself much more than against others. In a short while, pilots would have a fraction of a second to use the speed of the previous figure, to pull the control surfaces or the trapeze with the necessary dexterity, to feel the reaction of their hang glider when 'going inverted' or doing a spin, to prepare the exit heading, and remember the next manoeuvre. This was a meeting face to face with the present, almost a way of stopping time.

One forgot about the competition and sought perfection in every movement. It was this state of total concentration that sixteen aerobatic pilots were trying to reach, in the strange atmosphere that prevailed the site.

Then, the takeoffs begin, one after another. Colourful shapes whirled above the sea. The traces of smoke died out but the images were engraved in the pilots' eyes. Every figure was different, each programme was empirical: this was still art. Finally, on the beach, technical matters re-gained the ascendancy. Straight after the landing, questions and commentaries would flow, joys and disappointments would show, reminding us that this was a competition at a European level, with its organizational imperatives and regulations.

The first day ended as expected: a dual between flexible wings and rigid wings with three-axis control. I was at the head of the intermediate ranking with my rigid ASW Flash, ahead of Didier's Mirage followed by two flex-winged hang gliders. Two flying styles had emerged already. Didier perfectly mastered very wide loops and flat spins, while I preferred to do sequences of movements, holding precise headings, and to stick to the programme announced. Most competitors set very high standards and the jury had a hard job to decide.

The first round of the following day narrowed the gap even further. The movements were of breathtaking quality. But of course, the basic level was the loop!

The last round was marked by saturation. The heat was stifling, everyone was tired. Didier missed the beginning of his programme and it took him several seconds to start his spins, which made him lose many points. I took off feeling so sure that I would keep the title won the previous year, that I lost concentration. I had to locate the axis, empty my mind for an instant despite stage fright, gain some speed by pulling my trapeze to the stop. The hang glider reached 70 mph, I could feel it through the vibrations of the structure. I released the traction of the trapeze, the hang glider straightened up, I pushed a bit more, then against the stop: a first loop, a speed increase, control bar to the right, I pushed again: a wingover followed by reduced speed to enter a series of deliberate spins; I reached 4 or 5 G, this was the most physically trying stage. Three turns, then I released the control bar abruptly to end lined up with the axis while keeping my speed for the next loop. I pushed once, the hang glider slowed down and made a low-speed comma-shaped loop, leaving me weightless. Because of the low airspeed, I drifted sideways, making me lose my exit heading. For a while, I didn't know where I was and automatically moved on to the next loop, completely off centre. I was too low down, spatially disorientated and had lost track of my programme. I interrupted it and landed on the beach. Too self-assured, I had lost concentration through exhaustion and an excess of self-confidence, losing touch with my perception of the air and of my movements. I also lost my top place in the final ranking.

If it is difficult to be fully conscious of the flight while doing acrobatics, it is even more difficult to juggle with it during each task. Consciousness cannot be acquired once and for all, it has to be recovered every time. This may be the reason why some flights end up in disaster, and also why some excellent pilots sometimes give up aerobatics for long periods of time. In any case, it proves the interest of this discipline, which relies on the human aspect beyond technique itself.

While society life in Monaco was at its height, pilots and organisers were saying goodbye; they had spent a weekend in a delicate and intangible space, where sensitivity, subtlety and achievement had sculpted the sky with traces of orange smoke.

I like these arabesques. They are all different but they often transmit the same emotion, the same desire to seek new challenges.

They give us access to an incredibly rich world, connecting us to our deepest inner resources. These are the traces we have to follow. Straight lines remain on the same plane, they do not take you to another dimension.

CAPE SUNION:

WHERE TIME IS ETERNAL

Brushing against years of history with the tips of our wings

HERE I WAS, THROTTLE RIGHT OPEN, full power on, standing on the brakes. The front wheel began to slide across the sand; I brusquely released the aircraft which shot forward. Our improvised runway was tiny, some 25 yards long by 2 yards wide. A slight cross-wind was coming from the sea. One of the back wheels hit a grassy mound, projecting the hang glider to the right then another grassy mound sent it back to the left. I risked my all and pushed at arm's length: my 50 HP literally lifted me off the ground. I hadn't kept my heading properly. The heat of the Greek summer was stifling, we felt overpowered by the sun. Fortunately, as a safety precaution, we had decided to take off alone on our two-seaters. My friend Christian left a few seconds before me in a cloud of sand. We met again, forming a tight formation, a few yards above a glassy sea. We had just taken off from a beach some 30 miles from Athens with only one thought, not to say an obsession: to fly over Cape Sunion and the temple of Poseidon at sunset, but in our own aircraft, without a helicopter or any special privileges! I had been dreaming of doing this since my first trip to Greece when I was 14, and had told Christian about it.

For the first time ever, some microlights were going to fly over a site which had witnessed 2500 years of History. But we no longer thought of it as an achievement; the only thing that mattered that

53

day was the communion of our Dacron sails with the blocks of marble, of our aluminium tubes with the columns which had stood up to twenty five centuries of storms. Our frailty seemed to dominate the temple. We absent-mindedly greeted a few tourists who regarded our aircraft as the future of aviation. In fact, we were only thinking of the past... and living the present.

I knew that my dream was only going to last two gallons worth of fuel. I could hear Lamartine implore[1]:

"Oh time, adjourn your flight! And you, propitious hours,
Stop running away!
Let us savour the fast-going delight
Of our most beautiful day!"

And on that day, time answered my call: one hour of flying, one minute of piloting, and twenty-five centuries of emotions!

The sun was not quite touching the skyline. The stones were golden, like the century of Pericles. There, at the far end of Attica, the Athenians had built a fortress around the temple to dominate every move of their enemies and had placed it under the protection of the god of the sea. But that day, we were the masters of the place, it was our turn to dominate it... together with Poseidon.

I didn't even think about having to land on dry sand, rather difficult to pack down. The size of our take-off strip made it totally impossible for a landing : we would have to use the beach. I was only thinking of my flight and, in fact, I didn't need to think at all. Christian was holding his ultralight 15 feet away from mine. We were taking curves wing to wing. Nothing could trouble such a harmonious flight.

As the sun was going down, the columns turned red. The temple had been destroyed several times during the course of battle,

---

[1] Translator's note:
Excerpt from 'Le Lac' in *Méditations Poétiques* (1820) by French poet Alphonse de Lamartine (1790-1869).

engulfed in fire and blood. That evening, only the sun still bore traces of it. Our Pumas were acquiring its tones.

I cannot remember how many times I went round, passing close by antiquity again and again, brushing against years of history with the tips of my wings. I couldn't hear my engine; I heard storms and thunder, the cries of watchmen, the voices of oracles; I could see whole fleets of triremes coming towards the headland, towards 'our' headland; I could see warriors assaulting the sheer cliff.

The tourists had no idea. They had paid fifty drachmas for their ticket and could see us dream if they wanted. Every time I went past, a young woman waved her hand at me. Was she already there 2000 years ago? I waved back at her, she was beautiful. I was flying close enough to see that she was smiling at me radiantly. I loved her while the flight lasted, it felt like a century of beauty. I knew I would never see her again. I could not see her again or else the dream wouldn't be a dream anymore. Besides, gods are only regarded as gods when they are flying!

The sun continued moving away. A shroud of mist wrapped the ships which stood out against the horizon, in the infinity of the sea. The columns now looked black. The battle was coming to an end, leaving smouldering the remains of a civilisation our 20th century would never re-discover. Gone were the works of art, the tapestries, the sacrificial jewellery, but also our predecessors's daily life, their aims and their ideals. What was there of ours, in the materialistic era which we were coming back to?

Despite my fears of the back wheel having been bent during the violent takeoff, the landing was fine. The soft sand absorbed my Puma; I no longer wanted to move, no longer needed to. I implored Poseidon to let me stay for another twenty-five centuries, but I had to clear that improvised runway for Christian's landing.

That was all too far, in the future; the present had got hold of me and, as if against my own will, I continued to spiral over the headland, unable to detach my eyes from the timeless vision. The sun had disappeared, and with it the walls of the fortress which surrounded the temple. Eighteen columns were all that remained… Eighteen columns and two Pumas.

The sun sets over Cape Sunion every evening, but every evening is an eternity. I can now admit without shame that I cried that evening.

CASTLES IN THE AIR

Could the search for harmony be the key to the search
for Permanency?

NEXT TO THE WHITE FLOATS of my hydroplane-microlight, pictures of the Vabbinfaru and Thulhaagiri islands were unreeling
slowly. I was heading for Bandos, 'scraping' the surface of the
Indian Ocean. I had just started the engine again and switched off
the walkman after an hour's flight. It seemed only a day since Neil
Diamond had written his song for *Jonathan Livingston Seagull:*

"Lost on a painted sky, where the clouds are hanged for the
poet's eyes".

I played with small clouds hanging 5000 feet above the sea,
then cut off the engine and let my microlight fly by itself, against
the tropical sunset. In a few minutes, my aircraft would touch
water in the lagoon; I would describe my flight over a shoal of
dolphins I met on the way, the manta ray I escorted between the
reefs, the magnificent shades of the coral reefs and the volcanic
atolls which form the Maldives. In a few minutes, I would tell all,
but already I knew how to sum up the experience: I've seen castles
in the air!

And yet, on several occasions during the previous weeks spent
on Bandos, a 900-feet wide island, I almost changed the title of this
episode to 'Kikurani'. In the local dialect, a mixture of Indian and
African roots, *kikurani* means something like 'God, what shall I
do?' or 'What can I do about it?', expressing one's total impotence

before an incomprehensible or merciless fate. How many times did we hear this *kikurani*, dropped like a guillotine, when the petrol ordered the day before hadn't arrived, when all my spare parts were stolen from the airport customs premises, when the baksheesh given to the air company still wasn't enough to admit my aircraft into the baggage hold of the Boeing 737! We developed an aversion for this *kikurani* word until we realised that we, Europeans, were actually consumed by stress and the notions of time and money. For, after all, what did it matter if we had to wait for three weeks before my microlight got to the island? What did it matter if customs procedures lasted an hour or two days? What did it matter, in the end, if we flew that day or the next? Five weeks spent on Bandos were just enough to understand that, just enough to appreciate *kikurani,* just enough to wish it all lasted longer. We started laughing at the things that happened to us: the cook falling asleep on the bread instead of preparing our sandwiches; the room-service waiter taking the ice-cream out of the freezer half an hour early, despite the ambient temperature of 104°F and pretending it was still frozen; the notice on the door of the dentist's surgery (1 hour away from Bandos) reading: 'We are very sorry but our drill has broken down, we shall inform you as soon as it is repaired'! The said dentist, with only a year's training to his credit, had just attended a member of our group with some pliers in one hand and a torch in the other to pull his tooth out!

However, the idea behind the Maldives project wasn't to ponder over the different ethnical attitudes or to spend our time laughing about successive anecdotes. Our aim was to take some shots of these heavenly islands from a two-seater microlight for a feature film… which never came out: *kikurani*?!

True enough, problems had started in Switzerland. Our microlight was to pass in transit through Sri Lanka. At the last minute, a Swiss civil-servant stopped the loading process, declaring that 'military material couldn't be exported to a country at war', all with a German Swiss accent and unshakeable seriousness! As a result, our crates had to be sent by freighter to Seoul, where more flexible laws allowed them to be returned to Colombo. This just proves that embargoes are merely a question of unnecessary miles… and a waste of time.

On top of the ten days reserved for the shooting, we had another three-week's wait, so, apart from carrying on with procedures, we also went to the beach and did some diving. We were in the kingdom of Herwarth Voigtmann, a diving instructor and photographer famous for his shark shows. We shot most of the underwater scenes for the film with him.

Diving by day and diving by night: the Maldives paradise was also underwater, but I could feel that Herwarth wanted to fly as much as we did. By the time Air Lanka unloaded our aircraft at Malé, we had almost given up on it.

The customs officer, seeing a microlight for the first time, went methodically over the whole structure and over the engine with his metal detector. Surprised by the continuous bleep of his machine, he switched it off thinking it had broken down! As a document was still missing, we had to wait until the next day to come and fetch my Puma, which meant another three hours by boat. What will always remain a mystery to me is the delivery note for Greek caviar which was attached to one of our crates!

To greet us back to Bandos, a crowd of natives led by a toothless elderly man was waiting for us. Lifted by a few dozen arms, the microlight was unloaded from the boat and assembled with a speed matching our impatience to fly. The elderly native quickly understood that the handling task was for the young and declared himself 'Chief Petrol', a nickname he probably still wears with pride. He was the man who brought us every day the petrol ordered two days before — or rather, the mixture of oil, dirt and fuel which we used to make the engine go, jamming the pistons in the process...

Two hours later, I left the port sailing on my floats; I couldn't wait any longer. I did a first takeoff alone to check the rigging. A kick on the rudder blade to align myself into the wind, throttle fully open, the microlight was riding the rungs, I gained some speed and took off... This time, I was flying over Bandos at last. I couldn't believe what I saw. The beauty of the atoll seen from above was breathtaking. The gradation of tones between the white sand and the deep sea covered all shades of green and blue. There were more islands than I had originally thought, each one surrounded with its coral reef. I was in the middle of a life-size picture postcard. I didn't prolong this solo flying because I knew some people on the beach were awfully envious. As I came back close to the shore, I could see Herwarth already waist-deep in the sea. He got into the second seat as soon as the blades of the propeller had come to a halt.

Even if the distance for the takeoff in a two-seater is over 200 yards, the climb rate is sufficient to play hide-and-seek with clouds. How fantastic it was to go through them as if threading some pearls on a necklace, to watch the islands disappear and reappear between each cloud, to admire the shadow of the wing circled with a small ring-shaped rainbow against the cotton-wool! It was so beautiful that I didn't keep an eye on the fuel consumption and we ran out of petrol! The boat that came to refuel my aircraft brought me another passenger and off we were again. This time, we came across a shoal of dolphins. Nature had packed so much beauty all in one place that it was like visiting an enormous amusement park. I started spiralling a few yards above the dolphins: they watched us go past with that quaint smile on their face. Before going back, we flew over some fishermen in a felucca, then made a sea-landing in front of our bungalows. The sea was fiercer than when we'd left. A particularly strong wave bent the whole of the front fork and we nearly overturned. This was only the first of a long series of DIY jobs. The person in charge of the generator on the island allowed me to search through a pile of scrap metal among which I found a few nuts and bolts in better shape than mine. As the repair was taking place on the water, my passenger and I took it in turns to dive and look for the tools, screws, nuts and bolts which inevitably slipped from our hands. Since my power drill and all my other tools were probably resting in the hut of one of the airport customs officers, we had to use our hands and some pliers to hold the bit in order to drill some holes in the stiffening tubes of the floats. Whilst we were at it, we also fixed some kind of support for the 35-mm camera which we would be using as from the next day.

The following night, we dreamed about islands, microlights and dolphins, but it didn't matter because the next day would be even more beautiful than any dream.

At 7 a.m , the engine was already on. Armed with four cameras, Herwarth and I had jumped out of bed to treat ourselves to a superb morning flight 5000 feet high, taking one shot after another, changing films and lenses in the air to make sure we didn't lose a single second of the show: a symphony of colours punctuated with morning clouds in the immensity of the Indian Ocean. After a sea-landing in the lagoon and a quick lunch, we moved on to another element, to get into the very world we had just flown over: Shark Point, 80 feet below the sea. Birds gave way to fishes. Herwarth tapped his knife against a bottle to attract some sharks that were 6 or 7 feet long. He then proceeded to feed them from his hand, and from his mouth. Countless numbers of colourful fish surrounded us. We played with a few spiny lobsters and stroked a big moray, delighted to have its head scratched to get rid of its sand fleas. The most fearsome predators seem to become harmless as soon as men give up their instinct of domination to genuinely blend with their environment, their universe. Freedom was the only element we knew then, and, between currents, we did all the figures of aerobatics. A three-dimensional space with an added sensation of being with oneself. I even managed to overcome my claustrophobia and entered a submarine cave full of 'lion-fish', a type of fish with dreadfully poisonous spines. Our communion was so perfect that I had followed Herwarth (almost) without hesitation.

When all the air from our bottles had been turned into movements and fascination, we went back up to take off again. This time, our altitude was limited by the danger of excessive depressurisation just after a dive, so we decide to take some shots hedgehopping, or rather 'island-hopping'. Here was an opportunity to test the different settings for the 35 mm camera and expose the first reels. It was also an opportunity to give Chief Petrol his first flight. Dressed in a pareo, the elderly native was trying not to show signs of panic before the youths that awaited him on the beach, full of admiration. After a tour round the island endured bravely, he couldn't wait for me to take him back to the pontoon and jumped out as soon as we had landed. I wonder if his friends believed him when he got back to the shore, completely soaked, his few teeth chattering, and declared proudly:

"No problem!"

In fact, I was the one who was having problems. A short-circuit caused by sea water had created a live contact between the structure of the wing and the engine through the ignition switch: the electric shocks I got in my arms sometimes prevented me from holding the trapeze with the gas on! If Chief Petrol had known this, he would probably have jumped out well before the landing!

A quick DIY job isolated the electric circuit, but we had other problems. During a flight with a tourist – who took it in his stride, being English – the engine suddenly died out. A few days before, a driving belt had snapped, a hand towel had lodged itself in the propeller, and, due to a moment of inattention, I had forgotten to open the fuel valve. But this was different. There was nothing abnormal except that the engine had stalled and wouldn't get going again, even though I pulled hard on the starter. The only reassuring thing was that the 'landing site' was big enough! We landed in the open sea and began to drift, pushed by a strong wind. In front of us, there was only one island separating us from the coral reef, the Indian Ocean and… Australia. Just as we were considering jumping into the water, for fear of turning into 'The Raft of the Medusa'[1], a current led us almost miraculously to the coast, of what was usually a desert island. We found a group of fishermen there… they had a transmitting set which enabled us to call Herwarth and be towed all the way to Bandos.

The diagnosis did not take long: a piston was perforated from side to side! Perhaps some dirt in the petrol, or some salt or sand in the carburettor? The spare 440 cc Fuji-Robin, brought by two natives carrying it in the middle of a pole like head hunters, was quickly assembled. If only I'd had time to go and fetch my camera, taking a snapshot of the scene would have cheered me up a little.

We spent the rest of the day running the new engine in, and on the morrow we were ready to face the next problem cheerfully. The wind was too strong, the rudder blades too small: the microlight was uncontrollable on the water, it kept on going into the wind. Just as the engine stalled, my passenger (another one!) had no choice but jump into the water to prevent us from crashing against the reefs which ran along the small harbour. Half drowned and grazed by coral, he endeavoured to protect the floats from total destruction while I was holding the hang glider to make it catch the wind a little.

---

[1] Painted in 1819 by French artist Théodore Géricault, the picture shows the sinking of the Medusa in 1816, off the coast of Western Africa. Out of the 149 souls who had sought refuge on a raft, only 15 dying men were found 12 days later.

A tourist rushed towards us but we soon became disillusioned when we saw him stand in the water to get his camera out. He mistook the waving of our hands for a greeting, which increased his delight in taking pictures of the first microlight he had ever seen.

Anyway, after almost drowning, we had to repair the floats and let the fibreglass dry for forty-eight hours. As a precaution, I'd had some stuff brought over from Switzerland in case repairs were needed. Apart from this order, made through radiotelephone at a cost of 9 euros per minute, I had managed to send a few words of love to Michèle. She hadn't been able to stay in Bandos until the delivery of the microlight, which was delayed because of that stupid Swiss civil servant already mentioned. If only I had landed with her on a desert island!

While the polyester solidified, the underwater festival could be resumed. A particular night dive has crystallised in my memory. In the film script, there was a scene where the Prince falls off his sinking ship and is found by the Little Mermaid. When the actor jumped from the boat, the Moon and the stars entered the sea like a cloud of sparks. We were crouching at the bottom with the cameras and the spotlights. The cold was biting my skin but I felt great; I liked this union between sky and water, light and darkness, being surrounded by sleeping fish and beating hearts. Then came a shower of gold and jewels from the smashed chests drifting from the ship. The corals glittered as in daylight, the cameras were running, the Little Mermaid was about to save the young Prince. I fell in love with the moment, with the place; above all, I felt grateful to all that had led me there and to all that would allow me to describe it later. Telling a story is a kind of prolongation of a given moment; that's probably why I like writing.

I had already begun to feel how my Maldives experience had me torn between dreams and reality, between ecstasy and brutal awakening. This is why, when getting back to the surface, I wasn't

"A childhood between the Earth and the Sky."

"The circle had revolved, but it was always the same circle. I was beginning now to perceive the centre of it."

"A relationship in which 1 + 1 = 3 consists of regarding communication as comparing experiences rather than sharing ideas."

"Ariadne's thread which my mother helped me to preserve."

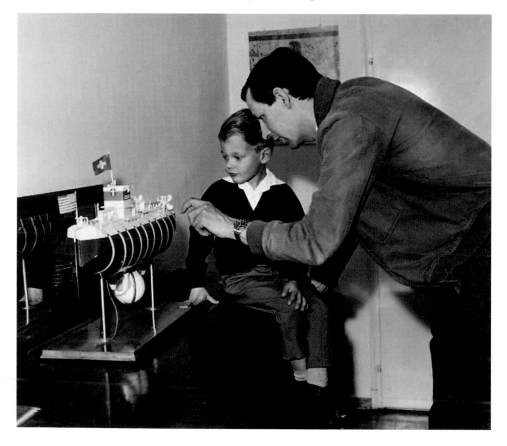

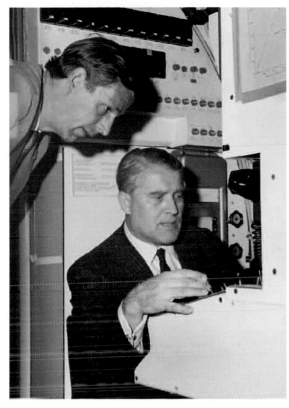

"It was easy to represent the third generation when I had a whole life ahead of me to do everything.' Here with Wernher von Braun, the father of the NASA space programme, and astronauts Scott Carpenter (Mercury 4) and Bill Anders (Apollo 8)."

"I suddenly felt transported back to the same place, at a time when I was a candid and naive 12-year-old boy dreaming of becoming an explorer."

"...Breitling Orbiter 3 was sitting imposingly among the strange and marvellous aircraft of my childhood heroes". (Apollo 11 capsule, the Wright Brothers's aeroplane, Charles Lindbergh's Spirit of St. Louis, and Chuck Yeager's supersonic X1.)

"I used to think that I had to choose between family tradition and medicine, without knowing yet that medicine is also a way of exploring Life".

altogether surprised to find myself in the middle of an oil slick, probably left by some leaky tanker. But the black dirt on our skin didn't take the shine away from our eyes!

A shine that would last all the more since, on the next day, we were filming the kingdom where the Prince had been shipwrecked. The flights at a high altitude were followed by hedgehopping ones. The camera was fixed at the far end of the dolly and the cameraman had to lie flat on his stomach over the first seat while I was piloting from the rear one. The centre of gravity was so displaced forward that the trapeze was blocked and any adjustment of the altitude had to be done by controlling the throttle. We had become stuntmen out of necessity, but we were having such a great time that we didn't have the slightest bit of vertigo.

The flight continued for several hours, during which I saw my small paradise go through all possible shades of colours from sunrise to sunset. The scene was set on the beach and some feluccas were requisitioned from fishermen. I whirled from one island to the next, from a shoal of dolphin to a manta ray, and we used up several 35 mm reels, until the beginning of a storm on the last day. To meet with the requirements of the film, I tried one takeoff too many and was brutally called back to reality when a wave tore off the front support of the floats. The microlight went nose-down and we had to use our bodies as counterweights to avoid capsizing. This time, the damage couldn't be repaired with what we had at hand. While the storm was getting nearer, we packed the material in the crates for the return journey. The wind tore what was left of the décor, leaving the landscape as devastated as we were.

Nevertheless, the images that went before my eyes while I was travelling from Malé to Zurich in a DC8 were quite different. Stripped to my swimming trunks and my helmet left at the far end of the bungalow, I was still feeling as if I was flying in my microlight.

The return to Switzerland was straight forward compared to the departure. Thanks to the impeccable service of a Swiss airline all my material was loaded as traveller's luggage with a ticket that was six times cheaper than Air-Lanka's! True enough, the airport baggage handlers probably had their part in it. When I placed the main 550 lb crate on their scales graduated up to 440 lb, they saw the needle going back to zero after doing a complete turn of the dial. I told them jokingly that my material was very light, but, to my disbelief, the foreman directing the natives wrote down 'zero kilo' on the freight list, before his twelve porters joined forces to load the crate on-board!

The captain had never carried another aircraft in the entrails of his aeroplane, which allowed me to make friends with the crew and spend a good part of the flight in the cockpit. We exchanged photos, shared some dreams. My head was still full of atolls and dolphins when we were flying over Lebanon and came across a military jet. Whether it was Israeli or Syrian, I don't know. It was flown by another human being, who took great pleasure in holding the joystick, yet he had probably dropped some bombs over an unknown target. In fact, several columns of smoke were visible below us. There was a war. When I met my fiancée at Zurich, maybe the napalm would still be burning. I remembered my twisted floats, my perforated piston, my stolen tools: what a load of trivia! While I was flying to feel alive, others were flying to kill. This was my first contact with war. Two days earlier, I had been carefree, playing with the small clouds that adorned my heavenly islands, at a four-hour flying distance (in a DC8) from Lebanon, now torn apart. The life of some doesn't prevent the death of others, just as war doesn't prevent people from being carefree. But when extremes clash too brutally, the usual judgement criteria are not enough. Things must be questioned for the sake of honesty.

On earth, paradise is next to hell. One goes with the other. They have to match, to complete one another, like the day and the night, summer and winter, left and right, the flower and the root… the yin and the yang. Outside divine Oneness, we are surrounded with duality, the whole of Creation is ruled by two opposing forces. Westerners seem to have forgotten what the Chinese have known for thousands of years. So where does man fit in all this?

In just a few hours, I had seen creation and destruction, joy and sadness, nature in full harmony and the Near East in complete madness. And there, from the cockpit of a DC8, I had the feeling that none of it was any use.

Horror has never made human beings want to give it up, and harmony has never made them yearn for happiness. Man is like a badly strung puppet. I had spent five weeks in a world where sharks and morays play with divers, where clouds are like pearls on a huge celestial necklace. Nature there is so beautiful that you think it's eternal. Yet, it's as fragile and short-lived as the happiness I had felt. So short-lived, in fact, that it may seem useless if you imagine horror afterwards. The harmony I'd experienced hadn't stop me from coming close to suffering: so what did that leave me with, apart from brief pleasure? That is, unless we reckon that our goal in life is to get as much pleasure as possible, which would be like collecting coins with only one side.

This is the sort of occasion when you get to wonder if God really exists. And if he does, how can he possibly allow so much suffering on Earth?

Wouldn't it be better to wonder, instead, why mankind keeps on ignoring the signs God has been sending us for thousands of years to show us how to reduce the suffering? All the prophets, all the initiated came back with the same message: terrestrial happiness is not an end in itself; the world in which we can blossom exists at another level, on another plane; a long spiritual effort is needed to reach it.

Perhaps you need to have suffered a lot to understand that.

As that song by Leonard Cohen says:

"And Jesus was a sailor

When he walked upon the water.

And he spent a long time watching

From his lonely wooden tower.

And when he knew for certain

Only drowning men could see him,

He said "All men will be sailors then

Until the sea shall free them".

If terrestrial life provided enough happiness, would anyone still be seeking God?

I found myself once again confronted with my oldest dream as a child: to stop the course of time in order to prolong intense moments. And it may be that, far from the films brought back from the Maldives, what enriched me most is this reflection: if a given moment cannot remain eternally in man's consciousness, there must be a form of consciousness that becomes permanent. Could the search for harmony be the key to the search for Permanency?

For a long time, believing in the theories of Karma and Reincarnation had made me accept the notions of good and evil; this would no longer be sufficient, I felt that personal experience resided in the present, not in some future terrestrial life; it resided in the spiritual work that reveals an immensely rich world inside us, to which we must be connected permanently. Only then can Man give a meaning to the yin and the yang… beyond the notion of opposites, through a vertical vision of Transcendence. This way, he will find his true place but also his responsibility: that of making the extremes touch, to be reunited with the Oneness to which he may aspire. This is how I understand these lines by the French mountaineer Jean-Michelin Asselin:

"The sky is the stage of the spiritual world,
The earth is the stage of the bodily one,
The Way goes through man's door".

From this viewpoint, pacifists lose as much energy to eradicate wars as ecologists do to preserve nature. Man's place is to be found beyond the extremes, in his search for Consciousness, for Permanence. Combining within himself both Hell and Paradise, a human being will then be able to make the long journey for which he was born.

COMING BACK FROM FAR AWAY

Opening up to life itself

HERE I AM, DRAGGING MY FEET, absorbed in my thoughts. Suddenly, life is taking on a new meaning, a crucial one. When you have been at the crossroad between life and death, all daily events become laughable and banal. I feel tired, off-beat, almost like an alien on earth, even guilty to have the same worries as 'before' since they now seem so trivial to me. 'Before' was up until last Saturday 6 p.m.. 'Before' was up until the last loop followed by a spin. 'After', is from the moment I landed, hanging from my emergency parachute. 'During', was...

I was feeling very calm and wanted to fly. The tow behind Alain's microlight had taken place in ideal conditions and I had just sent some smoke to leave a trace in the sky in tribute to my friend Patrice Barcouda. It was he who, two years earlier, had hauled me 15,000 ft above Lyons to establish a world record. It seemed only natural that I should take part in the annual show he organised in the Drôme valley.

The beginning of my programme oscillated between the cloudy blue sky and the lush green scenery. My first loop made my hang glider and my whole body quiver. I was happy. The spin was a little slow starting because I hadn't killed my speed properly after the wingover. I came out after one and a half turns, maintaining the dive for the next figure. All of a sudden, my Flash went faster and started vibrating. I immediately pushed the trapeze forward, to no avail. I knew from experience that this hang glider was unstable during a dive and that I had to persevere. But this time, I quickly realised that things were going to be different. The wing started porpoising, my suspension rope slackened and I lost control. The speed increased even further; the structure started to bend out of shape. I didn't dive at a very steep angle but the hang glider was falling faster than my body, which no longer acted as a pendulum. Much to my disgust, I would have to use the emergency parachute and the thought of my show being a disaster briefly assailed me. But just as I released my hand to pull on the handle, the whole hang glider started resonating and disintegrated into a tangle of tubes and cables.

The next fifty-five seconds are beyond description, beyond fear,… almost beyond life. It was like being a contorted puppet falling with the remains of a hang glider, spinning and swirling towards the ground. I was totally aware of what was happening, of being propelled at about 90 mph from a sky which seemed to spew me out. There was nothing I could do to stop the violence. The realisation that an action can be irreversible, that life can be lost in an instant, came to me like a heavy blow. And this time, it was happening to me. My face was very painful where a piece of the trapeze had probably hit me. My thoughts had disintegrated, I had lost all notions of time. Life or death depended on whether the Great Switch was set to the 'on' or 'off' position. There was no way I wanted to die, even if, for the first time in this life, there was a good chance it could happen to me. The rotation of the fragments centrifuged me in the middle of the sky amidst a vision I shall never forget, but which I cannot describe. In the middle of this vision, Michèle and Estelle, my six-month old daughter, appeared to draw me out of my numbing stupor. A sense of guilt overtook me for a while, that lasted an eternity. I didn't want to abandon them, I didn't want to admit that I was crashing; I rejected this situation which proved that acrobatics in a hang glider are dangerous, very dangerous, despite anything I had said to the contrary. However, I was not in a position to reject anything, I was fully aware that the situation was irreversible. I was falling in such disorderly movements and at such speed that I had lost any reference point in the sky.

Suddenly, like the whirling dervishes, of whose practice I had learned during spiritual retirement, I centred my mind upon myself, oblivious of what surrounded me, of the ground getting nearer and nearer, of the tubes hurting me. I was then able to find the handle of the emergency parachute easily. I had to take the small bag containing the canopy out of its container, and throw it as far away as possible. The container was stuck, I pulled like mad with my right arm while holding the smashed structure with the left one to keep my balance. Because of the centrifugal force, the bag escaped my grip and the strap unrolled. Everything I had seen or heard about this sort of situation crossed my mind. I knew I had to get hold of the strap to be able to free the canopy if it got tangled with the hang glider, but I couldn't find it. The fall continued, I couldn't see anything and seemed to be swimming in the air. I had never imagined that such brutality, such hell were possible. Words are pathetic when you realise you are about to crash into the ground, when you already sense within yourself the violence of the impact: everything is there, everything is present, all at once, in one single impression. I didn't see my life reel back, I didn't even cry, but I prayed aloud. It was one of those unreal atmospheres from which you have to wake up, like in a nightmare. It was hard to admit that it was the crude reality. You feel so impotent, it is unbearable.

Eleven seconds went by.

Suddenly, a shock followed by a decrease in the rotation had me hoping that the parachute had opened correctly. I hadn't caught sight of it since I'd pulled it out. After doing all I could to throw it, I'd hardly thought about it again. The fall was cushioned and I could see a small white dome with an orange stripe swinging slightly at the end of its yellow strap. A piece of the broken hang glider prevented me from seeing the rest of the sky. I found I was on my back, in my sail, with my feet up. I felt so relieved about the successful opening of the parachute that I forgot for a while that my head was still facing downwards. I could see simultaneously a vineyard and an electric line and several rows of trees traversing the land towards which I was falling, and there was no way I could guide my fall. After wriggling in my harness I managed to free my feet but one of my legs got caught in the cables. I had another flash: Here were the front stays, which were sheathed and had small ribbons on them to indicate the direction of the wind when you take off. I loosened them with my left hand to free my foot without tightening the buckle which held the shoe. I was now in an upright position and I found the strap at last. I clung to it, pushing away with my left hand a piece of the hang glider which kept on swinging against the parachute. Suddenly everything went silent; not a sound, but the earth was approaching rapidly. Everything below was green, I could no longer distinguish the wires or the trees. The wind pushed me away from the vineyard. Just two glances and the ground materialised. The landing was very hard, the crash resounded from my feet to my head and I collapsed among the remains of my hang glider.

Life then carried on. I could move my legs and arms all right; only my face was painful and I cleared some blood away. My guardian angel was busy today! Alain, who had watched the whole accident from his microlight, hedgehopped over me. I got up swaying to and fro and waved at him to reassure him, then fell down again. People rushed towards me, the ambulance arrived. They'd all had a great fright but their life would go on, while something had changed in mine. It was like coming back from far away, I would never be the same as 'before'.

Since then, I am dragging my feet, lost in my thoughts. My life seems both fundamental and trivial to me. I did all I could to preserve it, and after experiencing such a strong desire to survive, my daily motivations seem terribly banal. I went too far yet not far enough at the same time. I gambled with my life for the sake of a stunt flying show and I haven't even acquired the wisdom which this sort of experience ought to have given me.

Doubt assails me: after extolling the virtues of being confronted with risk, all of a sudden I'm not sure if the things I wrote in this book are right. I seem to be going round in circles. I managed to get out of a difficult situation because I was familiar with aerobatics but the only reason why I had found myself in that situation was because I did aerobatics! In life, there are times of doubt, periods of crisis, without which we would be deluded with a permanent feeling of certainty. The ancient Chinese knew it full well. Far from moaning about the doubts which arise in such moments, they represented the word 'crisis' by combining the ideograms for 'danger' and 'luck'.

The day after my accident, as I got into a microlight again, I felt like a beginner, a bit as if I had completed a sixteen-year cycle which brought me back to the starting point. But I saw life from a different angle, or rather I saw two lives: the every day one in which we waste so much energy trying to forget the second one, which is essential because of the way it relates to a world beyond us. And now I felt guilty still to be giving importance to trivialities when I'd got a taste of what was essential. I could have struggled for thirty-two years to become rich and famous, but on that Saturday, at 6 p.m., I wouldn't have taken any of it with me. At least, nothing but the work carried out until then to try and understand the meaning of life – since it may be that a certain form of consciousness lingers after death.

I had learned to control, in the intensity of the present moment, all that could be controlled. However, there are a great many things you cannot control! Big chunks of our existence remain incomprehensible and mysterious to us. I hadn't done enough flights in a hot-air balloon to know that all this could be explored as well...

By getting more and more fascinated with risk, I've had the opportunity to slowly grasp a few basic values and to keep only one in mind in the end: living. But living with another aim than 'before'. Not just flying to feel that I am flying, but to live to feel that I am living. This didn't mean I had to give up on my wildest dreams, but to stand back from them and allow myself to laugh at them from time to time.

If in the past I had followed Ariadne's thread to the cosy and marvellous atmosphere of a child awakening to the world, after this accident, I followed it to the moment of my awakening to life itself. But now I felt like a complete alien compared to those who seem to forget that the very act of living is vital and miraculous.

The very idea of existing contains the crossroads where our individual paths meet. Without being aware of it, we share the same existence, as if we all drank the same water from the same stream. This is something we too often forget; as a result, differences and conflicts get the upper hand over harmony, human beings forget the meaning of Love. Indeed, what is Love for others, if not the consciousness of following an identical path, each in our own way, more or less well, more or less easily. Starting from a common source and going towards the same unknown goal. This implies a good deal of humility and tolerance towards our successes, our errors and our failures.

It's easy to love somebody rich or brilliant, whose company is pleasant to us; but is this the kind of love religions all talk about?

When you feel that you are sharing with others the most valuable thing in the world, you are then able to love them beyond their outer aspect, even if you don't like them. A given behaviour may be hateful, a given personality may be detestable, but we are all following our difficult path, with the means we have, the best we can – most of the time without understanding how we got to where we are. I have sometimes managed to see from that angle people who had harmed me, or criminals who had come to my practice. Each time, this different perception gave me a feeling of liberating grace, a bit as if loving somebody truly was of direct benefit to us, making us aware of our true place in this world.

I still haven't fully understood how much of my life will change as a result of this experience. When writing these lines, I don't even know if I am going to do acrobatics in a hang glider ever again. But I know I have to grasp the opportunity to understand a little better the meaning of Life. It may be that through the extreme flights carried out at air shows, I succeeded in liking myself enough to now be able to truly love others, in the stream of life which carries us all. And from now on, when I walk dragging my feet, I'll know that I could be walking far away, because that's where I came back from.

SCIENCE AND INTUITION

A world beyond our perception

IN THIS BOOK SO FAR, I've been travelling between ocean depths and Alpine summits, between modern technology and ancient ruins, with those who accepted the invitation to follow me. But beyond places and time, I followed the course of my thoughts, making a few halts here and there to consider a variety of topics such as risk, destiny, consciousness, permanency. Yet I didn't intend to write a philosophical book. On the contrary, I limited myself to mentioning a few experiences because I think that life itself is the most beautiful book, the most fabulous training ground, provided you live your life to the full. Nor did I intend to demonstrate the correctness of my ideas, I only wanted to express them. Trying to prove things may be greatly reassuring but it kills intuition; it destroys the spark which could prompt us to question ourselves, to ask ourselves:

'What if there was something else beyond certainty?'

I am sometimes wary of the sciences which rely purely on calculations and intellectual reasoning as a source of knowledge. That deprives us of any possible discovery in 'immeasurable' fields and it leads us to believe only in what we see, in the tip of the iceberg. For some scientists, a phenomenon can only exist if it has been duly measured and demonstrated. In my life, on the contrary, you have to show me that something doesn't exist before I stop believing in it. In a way, this is Pascal's challenge transposed onto the study of Life in general.

Indeed, it seems to me that we have much to gain by considering the possible existence of unexplained phenomena, of natural laws which are beyond us, keeping our mind open as a result. Intellectual reasoning is but a portion of the process of discovery, complementary to intuition. I love this sentence by the mathematician Euler: "Science is what you do after you guess right". While in the past there was a certain lack of scientific approach, I believe that, right now, we should reassert the value of having a developed intuition. I am always startled to see how people languish in their rigid views of the world, refusing to be open to other currents of thought; how they feel reassured by sticking to their so-called certainty, instead of developing their receptivity and opening their mind to what is beyond them. It's a bit like deciding not to open a chest full of diamonds, just because you don't like the shape of the key.

This doesn't make me gullible or naïve. I'm simply interested in another frame of mind. When interviewing me, people often ask me whether I believe in such or such thing. I don't think it's important to settle for one faith or another, given that your ideas change as life goes on; the important thing is to be prepared to go beyond your own sensibilities, to be prepared to believe the unbelievable, to accept the unacceptable. You have to give up clinging to what you think is crucial in order to enrich your life continuously with a taste for discovery; to breakaway from routine in order to have access to a different world.

But even though my approach is different to my father's or my grandfather's, I feel that my craving for exploration is part of the family tradition. Neither of them accepted that man should content himself with living on the firm ground, and they explored the sky and the sea. The limits of science have been pushed back, but they are still limits. I reckon that, deep down, I reject these limits. I don't content myself with the earth, the sky and the sea. Man must be able to discover another, even more fascinating world, by going beyond the usual limits.

Freedom isn't gained by pushing frontiers back. It doesn't consist in flying higher and higher or in diving deeper and deeper, it consists in feeling that you are flying, in feeling that you are diving. It doesn't consist in living as well as possible, it consists in feeling that you are alive, in knowing what and why you are living. True freedom can only be internal: that's the only type of freedom which external events cannot take away from us.

Yet, when I started hang gliding it was some kind of freedom I was seeking at first. During my first takeoffs, when discovering high altitude flights, when climbing in thermals and circling with eagles, when looping the loop at sunset, when in a sky full of hot-air balloons, or between Bandos and Thulhaagiri, every time, I thought to myself that this was true freedom at last. In fact, I was confusing freedom with fascination.

A little honesty forced me to admit that, whether in the air or on the ground, we are all subjected to external constraints. It might sound shocking, but I reckon that we don't act but 'react' freely. The weather forecast dictates whether I'm hang gliding or going to the cinema; during a flight, it is the thermal currents, the landscape, the obstacles, the laws of aerodynamics which condition my happiness; what makes me smile or pull a face is the degree of satisfaction I get from my usual pleasures. If I'm not aware of them, external circumstances will decide for me, and my faith in some utopian freedom will prevent me from seeing the mechanical aspect of my daily life. By trying to free myself, I first discovered what a slave I was.

Yet, if we are not free to 'do' as we want during a flight, we are free to 'be', to live in a particular state, and we are also free to continue seeking that state after the landing.

A discourse like this would have seemed absurd to me fifteen years ago. Now that I've tried to feel free through all possible means in the air, I realise that the notion of freedom is very different to what I had originally thought, less spectacular too. The word 'freedom' is one of the most deceitful terms of the human language. It justifies pressing on regardless, struggling against nature, rebelling against your destiny or even going to war against your neighbours, but it very rarely makes you question your own functioning, your own nature.

Nevertheless, the mechanical aspect of human life may be perceived through psychoanalytical approaches. For example, we know from the beginning of the 20th century that man's psyche is made of a conscious part and a subconscious one, and that the analysis of this subconscious allows us to understand our desires, our reactions, our way of relating to others, in short, our every day behaviour. Therefore, our personality is, in some way, the result of everything we have lived until now, either voluntarily or not. This leaves us with few opportunities to change our existence, except for those big crises which hit us from 'outside'.

The major contribution of philosophers such as G.I. Gurdjieff lies in the fact that ordinary consciousness isn't presented as an optimal function, but, on the contrary, as a state of lethargy, of dependence on the surroundings and on our mechanical thoughts, in contrast with a real Awakening which one could call 'Hyperconsciousness'. If analysing our subconscious helps us to understand our personality, it seems that the perception of our 'Hyperconsciousness' would allow us to approach the mechanism of what transcends us.

Since scientific thinking no longer has the means to dissect this 'Overconsciousness', since it cannot grasp its coherence in terms of causality or law, it labels it as a story for simpletons, an esoteric message for a chosen few or, on a good day, a nice little oriental tale.

However, life is strewn with signs and messages proving the existence of a world which is beyond us: explanatory or premonitory dreams, so-called 'coincidences', 'chance' meetings, flashes of lucidity, contacts made at the right time with new ideas, with the symbolic remnants of original Traditions. Carl Gustav Jung wrote "these coincidences in time of two or more causally unrelated events which have the same meaning or a similar one" and called them 'synchronicity', or 'meaningful coincidences'. From this perspective, we could regard astrology as the study of the synchronicities between the planetary cosmos and the human microcosm. The I Ching, in turn, would be the simultaneous manifestation of universal laws appearing both in the state of open interrogation of the subject and in the sticks of the game.

Another way of looking at it would be to feel that there is no causal effect linking the events of our life but only simultaneous manifestations of a same Whole, governed by the same Meaning. In other words, we usually look for the cause of what happens to us when we cannot find the meaning of it, at the risk of rejecting everything that seems improbable in terms of causality. I had an interesting example of this after flying over the temple of Poseidon in a microlight.

During the course of a conversation on this topic, a friend of mine, who had already impressed me with her remarkable knowledge in astrology, asked me if I'd had a particular experience in June 1983. She had noticed on my birth chart that, at the time, Neptune was passing through my 12th house in conjunction with the native Saturn. As it happens, Neptune is of crucial importance to me, since it rules my Ascendant. As I realised that Neptune was the Latin word for the Greek god Poseidon, I remembered the flight over Cape Sunion on 28th June 1983. I was stunned with the synchronisation of what had taken place at two different levels: while I was meeting Neptune and taking photos of his temple from a microlight, a similar meeting was taking place on another plan, in my birth chart, a kind of 'photo' of my sky. The position of Saturn in the 12th house even explained the way I had described the experience. Such configuration could lead me to (and I'm quoting) 'give a concrete form, either visual or auditory, to subconscious images or internal pressure': entirely composed in my head during the flight, the text about Cape Sunion was transcribed all in one go that same evening.

No mediaeval alchemist who knew the Emerald Tablets would have been surprised at my experience, since he would have been familiar with this quote, apparently inspired from the Taoist cosmology:

'That which is above is as that which is below; that which is below is as that which is above, in order to perform the miracle of Oneness.'

While listening to my astrologer friend, I could not but feel fascinated with such clear application of one of those apparently hermetic laws: what had taken place in my astral sky had also taken place in the sky at Cape Sunion: a meeting between Saturn and Neptune. Of course it was not because of my birth chart that I had flown over Cap Sunion on 28th June 83, but it so happens that I'd lived the same thing simultaneously on two different planes, a practical and tangible plan and a subtle, intangible one, which can be 'photographed' nevertheless... on my birth chart.

And yet, isn't this correlation between what is above and what is below totally obvious? If we think a little about what surrounds us, all the links in the chain ranging from the smallest to the biggest, from the atom to the cosmos, are built in a similar way. They are probably governed by the same universal laws; not those we think we know, but those we could get to know. The notion of microcosm ceases to be a theoretical and metaphorical vision when you observe its similarities in the universe. Atoms, like the solar system, are made of particles (electrons or satellites) which gravitate in an orbit around a central nucleus. Human beings are also made of a physical nucleus surrounded with energetic layers similar to the orbits of electrons. Even medicine is beginning to admit that man doesn't have one but two bodies, the physical one and the energetic one. The most advanced research in modern physics now agrees with the most ancient conception of cosmology. People are now talking again of the equivalence between matter and energy, between the very small and the very big, and maybe they'll soon accept again that Man, through his observation of extremes, is the link between them. Then the alchemical quest will come back to favour. After all, it consisted in searching for – or even welcoming – God in the inner self through the study of universal laws and their analogical application on the largest and the smallest scales. Transforming your inner life into a divine dimension as one would turn base metal into gold.

If alchemy, of which astrology is a pillar, fascinates me, it is because it integrates physics, psychology and spirituality in a triad to explain the meaning of Things.

True enough, like many Cartesians, I could have rejected these notions from the start. Then I would never have discussed astrology with that friend, and I would have been the loser. Nor would I have understood that the difference between a horoscope in the newspaper and a genuine birth chart is the same as between a pocket calculator and a computer.

I wouldn't have been able to feel that human beings are part of a Whole, that they are governed by laws which are beyond them and whose perception increases their consciousness instead of limiting their freedom; that there are billions of stars similar to our Sun, but that man still thinks he's at the centre of the universe.

Some thoughts give you vertigo and too many badly phrased questions can cause depression or anguish – whatever the level of these questions, and even more so when they deal with the meaning of Life. It's easier to close your eyes, to sever the ties which may

85

be linked to the unknown, and seek refuge in safe moral dogmas, whether scientific or religious. People find it more reassuring to chase the mirages of daily life, never mind if all this hot air disappears when we die.

Some questions will always remain unanswered, they will always be the cause of mental illnesses or escape from reality, unless a spark of lucidity prompts us to seek beyond prejudice, beyond the desert we have to cross to acquire a more global Knowledge. Indeed, it is often when we are in deep doubt, cut off from usual references, and with every reason to believe all is lost, that what I would call the 'rupture' takes place. A rupture from the pre-established pattern of existence, from sadness and anguish, from the fear of nothingness. A rupture in the continuity between a world we know and another which contains solutions. A rupture which generates open-mindedness, new visions and an evolution.

This 'desert' may be the mental space in which physical or psychiatric patients withdraw for years, rejecting what life has to offer them and struggling to go back to their previous state, or, it may be the state of the open and questioning mind of the Buddha in meditation. But for those who are neither ill nor a Buddha, the sudden realisation that you don't know anything anymore, as described by Socrates, may be the opening to a certain form of wisdom. Then doubt becomes a precursory sign of a different, direct form of knowledge: intuition.

For my part, I've had the opportunity to get the sensation of being out of my depth on several occasions, especially during spiritual retirement, when I had to brusquely abandon all the pre-established ideas I'd brought along; letting go of things could only be achieved after harrowing doubts had assailed me for several days; then I would gradually become sensitive enough to gain access to a more subtle understanding of Life. But I think that the strongest experience took place during my mother's funeral. Overwhelmed by the impression that nothing made sense anymore and that nothing could really make me feel better. Suddenly, beyond despair and almost in spite of myself, I felt an unexpected strength which filled me with serenity.

It seems that it is only through the permanent questioning of certainty that, feeling his way, Man will be able to discover his place in the universe. With a little humility, he will be open to the forces and the laws which govern the cosmos he belongs to.

And then questions will be answered...

Yet, that day, when I looked at the remains of my hang glider broken in a recent accident, I found no explanations or answers. I wasn't even sure whether to resume aerobatics. I didn't grasp the meaning of what had happened to me and went into a period of doubt like those I had known before.

One of my life cycles had come to an end. It was time to move on to something else, but I didn't know it yet. I desperately tried to organise a microlight expedition to Egypt, to no avail. All my projects and intents were a failure, one after the other; I eventually gave up with a heavy heart.

Instead of devoting my time to air expeditions as I had done so far, I focused on my training as a psychiatrist, which had become more important. My wife even remarked that I was beginning to talk of my consultations (within the limits allowed by medical confidentiality) with the same enthusiasm as when I told her about my flights.

Then, one evening, through one of these tricks which destiny has in store for you, something unbelievable took place. Because of an insignificant detail, my life was to change completely and all that had happened before would make sense.

Arriving late at the pilots' banquet in Château-d'Œx, I took the only free seat that remained in a room holding four hundred people. It so happened that the man sitting next to me was Wim Verstraeten, a Belgian pilot who had launched me from his balloon two or three years earlier. The topic of conversation rapidly moved to a project for a transatlantic race launched by Cameron Balloons and the Chrysler car makers. The idea was to commemorate the 500th anniversary of the discovery of America by Christopher Columbus, organising a historic race from the United States to Europe between several balloons. Being a Cameron hot-air balloons dealer, Wim had been selected and he had to find himself a team mate.

'You ought to take Bertrand with you, said the woman next to him. Having a doctor on board would be ideal.'

'Indeed, it would be an excellent idea to have a psychiatrist by my side, said Wim, already calculating the importance of human factors in this type of expedition.'

Exactly sixty years had passed since my grandfather had flown into the stratosphere with a Belgian team mate, sponsored by the National Fund for Scientific Research in Belgium. What a superb commemoration it would be if I could fly with Wim!

Nevertheless, I felt disconcerted by this project. I was used to flying into the wind, to control my hang glider to the last fraction of an inch by feeling the wind in my face, to chose my route and my landing site. And all of a sudden, I was invited to accept being pushed by the wind 16,000 ft above the ocean, without any real means to direct my course. When you fly in a balloon, you know full well where you come from, but you have no idea where you're heading for! Flying with the wind is like entering into a crisis voluntarily. Like losing control and being led towards the unknown. Did I really want that? Moreover, as the balloon moves exactly at the same speed as the air mass that propels it, you keep on thinking you've stopped. As a hang glider expert, I shouldn't have been seduced by Wim's suggestion; but given the period of doubt I was going through, was I still a hang glider expert?

I was fascinated with the history of the Northern Atlantic, that immensity which separates the Old from the New World and which, until 1492, had kept millions of Westerners wondering about what it concealed. After Christopher Columbus, successive waves of adventurers had crossed it, looking for a new life, for a mythical El Dorado. Then history had continued with the challenge of the Blue Ribbon, with Charles Lindbergh, but also with fourteen failed intents to cross it in a hot-air balloon, until the victory of *Double Eagle II* in 1978.

I was going through one of these moments in life when destiny depends on a yes or no answer. I could have said no. I could have refused that invitation and persisted in my obstinacy to fly into the wind. But I said yes, out of faith and for the pleasure of discovering something different to what I already knew. The next months were going to provide me with some signs that confirmed I had taken the right decision.

While on a trip to Shanghai to study the different aspects of traditional Chinese medicine, I wandered through an antique shop during my spare time. I came across a collection of those talismans and medals which the Chinese used to be so fond of. Without really knowing why, I took a coin and asked the salesman to translate the four ideograms on one of its sides. To my greatest surprise, he started saying:

'When the wind blows in the same direction as your path...'

I had already bought the coin before the startled salesman had time to finish:

'... it brings you great happiness.'

Where did this message come from, all of a sudden? After eighteen years flying with hang gliders and microlights, which needed to be facing the wind, to fly into the wind, and often involved a struggle against the turbulence and bumps of aerobatic figures, I was receiving a confirmation: it was now time to have the wind astern and accept being borne by the breath of Nature.

As a typical scientist, I could have combined the number of ideograms in Chinese and the quantity of medals made in China over the past two hundred years with the number of shops, in order to establish the likelihood of falling on this message by chance! And I wouldn't have learned anything! Rather than refuse to have an open mind and put forward any old statistical probability, I remembered a metaphor gleaned during a conversation:

'Chance is the language of the gods!'

Given the doubts inflicted on me by the remains of my hang glider had left me, it was clear that this message was an imperative answer, even if I ignored where it came from.

Later Wim would say to me:

"You'll end up making me superstitious!"

But what is superstition, to start with, if not the impression of lacking omnipotence; of being influenced by forces and universal laws above us, and which defy any scientific definition as a result.

As if to demonstrate that I had chosen the right path, that this talisman wasn't the fruit of probability, another spectacular synchronicity occurred as I was embarking for Bangor, the lift-off site for the transatlantic race. I arrived at the airport to join the rest of the Belgian team, with three items of luggage summing up the colours of the Belgian flag: black, yellow and red. Wim couldn't believe that I hadn't done it on purpose. Of course, as a psychiatrist, I first wondered if I hadn't done it subconsciously. But, as I reflected about it I saw that it wasn't so. I had taken the red suitcase because it was the biggest I had, and my sponsor had provided me with promotional bags, among which only the yellow one could be locked during the trip. As to the black one, my wife had brought it up from the basement at the last minute because the bag I was going to take originally was too small to hold the rest of my gear.

I clearly saw, in any case, that I had something important to do with Belgium that year. Enough to feel very confident and to understand why all the obstacles preventing my taking part in the Chrysler Challenge had spontaneously disappeared one after the other.

The reason why I like giving these examples is that I see in them a specific interface between the visible and the invisible world, between the state of lethargy in which we usually live and the state of true awakening in which the meaning of Life would become obvious. But the understanding of such phenomena has become almost impossible because we lack global vision. We don't often realise that events or sensations apparently isolated may be different manifestations of a same whole, just like the dots you look at with a magnifying glass form a complex figure once you look at them from the distance. We usually live on all fours, our nose stuck to the pattern of the rug which is our life, wasting our time giving importance to every detail. In theory, we could then define intuition as the capacity to stand back, to look for the links between the phenomena science cannot explain and to integrate them into a Whole. Intuition is what makes us want to know what visible or rational things actually hide behind them. By going beyond dogmas and sectarian or denominational ideas, the similarity of the different manifestations we can perceive is somewhat miraculous. Like a fourth dimension which brings together some apparently very different paths to make them converge into the same final goal, the same Meaning.

But I think that this realisation cannot take place alone, without hurt or suffering. It seems impossible to step back, to distance ourselves, without seeing the crude reality of the dreadful state in which we usually live. Like a house of cards, the illusions we were harbouring, the explanations which made us arbitrarily link the dots on the drawing, in short, the artificial references which made it possible for us to live almost blindly then collapse. Our system of values begins to totter and we sense that what we call free will and intention is in fact nothing but a series of more or less automatic reactions to the events we live, that love is often a mere process of identification with someone else, that freedom is accepted slavery and that morality is a generally admitted consensus. This is not ecstatic illumination but a painful observation. Not yet possessing the means to go further while refusing to step backwards is like being caught between the devil and the deep blue sea, and that can be unbearable.

Our ordinary state, a sort of self-effacement, is made possible by the illusory happiness of our brief stay on earth. It is strengthened by our denial of a superior Reality and protects us against this suffering. It drives us to reject at once the ideas which threaten our balance. Our defence mechanisms are often enough to ensure that we can continue being satisfied with our ordinary life. But sometimes, there are some 'flaws' which provoke either a spiritual evolution or depression or even madness. I think that this may explain some cases of psychosis brought on by some drugs. Indeed, how can you accept to leave your 'new paradise' once you've caught a glimpse, brutally and without preparation, of the state of delusion in which we normally live. How can you go back to the darkness of Plato's Cave when you have been exposed to sunlight? This is why drugs and other 'mystic short-circuits' are dangerous, and why all evolution has to follow its own rhythm, without us trying to smash up the reassuring scenery we set up as a protection against Reality.

But then, why spend so much energy in trying to change, if that leads to the uncomfortable situation of having lost everything without having gained anything else yet? It is precisely thanks to intuition that true Intention, genuine Love and a complete Freedom exist somewhere. It is also thanks to the intuition of another form of Knowledge, another state of Being, that we can sense things during the flashes of consciousness we are sometimes offered: like small lanterns being waved at us from the other side of the desert we have to cross.

More specifically, intuition can be experienced, can be felt deep within, during the moments of doubt or rupture which I have already mentioned, like a current of Life which obliges man to evolve. If science helps us to live our material life, intuition guides us to know how to live, how to listen, to decipher the landmarks of our existence, to find our way. If we listen with enough sensitivity, intuition will often provide us with some replies before we even need to formulate any questions.

Learning to live our life, and to find the way to a superior world is undoubtedly the raison d'être of the tests we all have to go through. That is, provided we don't choose to think that crises are entirely created by this cruel life to make us suffer. In fact, to remind us of our part of freedom, we have the Greek origin of the word crisis meaning 'decision'. It is up to us to decide what we want to do with what happens to us. Once we have lost the utopia of the terrestrial Paradise, driven to despair by the fragility of our happiness or the pain caused by our mortal condition, we can at last turn to other values by trying to go beyond our certainties, our prejudice and other internal limits.

Following a trace in the sky, from launches to loops, from the study of Chinese cosmology to the work of philosophers such as Gurdjieff and Krishnamurti, had brought me to focus on the study of man in general and medicine in particular. But to go even further, I needed to undertake something else. I needed to go into an unknown territory. I had to understand that doubt, crises and ruptures are the normal ingredients of a great adventure: the adventure of life itself. That's precisely what my experience with balloons would enable me to do.

WHEN THE WIND BLOWS YOUR WAY...
The unknown becomes your ally

A STEP INTO THE UNKNOWN, that's what the transatlantic race in a balloon was going to be, for me but also for all the other pilots invited by Chrysler: equipped with prototype balloons which had never flown before, ultra sophisticated electronic onboard apparatus which we had to test for various manufacturers, an empirical meteorological route planning system and above all, above all, 3000 miles of ocean to cross day and night. At this stage, the number of astronauts who had set foot on the Moon exceeded the number of balloonists who had crossed the Atlantic!

As for the crews, they were created artificially by the organisers, since in every kevlar capsule there was a Cameron balloon dealer and a co-pilot chosen essentially on media coverage criteria. The German crew consisted of Erich Krafft assisted by Jochen Mass, an ex Formula One champion. In the English team, Don Cameron was flying with Rob Bayly, a journalist, and in the Dutch one Evert Louwman, a European Chrysler representative, went with Gerhard Hoogeslag. The American balloon was manned by Troy Bradley and Richard Abruzzo, the son of Ben Abruzzo, who had been the first to cross the Atlantic: this journey back to the beginnings would turn out to be more than a mere adventure in the air for Richard. Wim Verstraeten had suggested I joined him aboard Chrysler 1, saying we would complement each other during the flight, but the organisers had probably paid more attention to my family background than to my qualities as a psychiatrist and a hypnotheratist!

We were due to lift off from Bangor, in the north-east of the United States. When we all got there, we soon stopped feeling like competitors. What the media regarded as a truly competitive race was totally upset by adverse weather conditions which delayed our departure for five weeks. Living in the same hotel and preparing together such a fascinating and perilous expedition could only lead us to be friends. The long wait, interrupted by false alarms and false hopes, influenced our state of mind so much that it would deserve being described at greater length. Since the organisers had decided not to inform us of the other balloons' position during the flight, we signed a pact (to their great displeasure): we would help one another by radio.

The daily briefing only contained bad news, and we had lost all hopes of ever lifting off when, one morning, the chief of mission, Alan Noble, rose the alarm for that same evening!

The organisers couldn't contain the excitement of the journalists and the public who had come to the big racecourse. Decorated with flags and small balloons, it looked like the venue for an American electoral campaign.

On our side, the unforgettable hours that followed were filled with emotion. I think that I later remembered every detail of the preparation, every thought, every movement. At last, we were doing all the gestures we had rehearsed and, after dreaming of the lift-off for five weeks, the atmosphere was really feverish. Yet, in front of us, all we could see was the black curtain of the dark night into which we had to merge.

Amidst the shrill whistling of helium taps, five big white masses began to tremble, to undulate on the ground, to liven up as more cubic feet of gas poured into them: we watched this magical show under the artificial brightness of the spotlights, our

"A new relationship will be created with nature, with birds, but especially with myself".

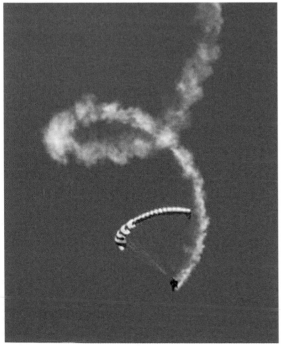

"The loop, that mythical figure in aviation where, for a moment, it isn't the Earth that revolves but man…"

"The word "vigilance" takes on a new meaning when our own life is in our hands…"

"From then on, we may discover an inner and unknown "dimension" which the requirements of daily life would not let us see. This 'dimension' consists of feeling that we exist not only within the action, but also within ourselves".

"I was beginning to feel that the path I had followed was a dangerous one, but as yet I didn't know with what it could be substituted".

"An opening to an unexpectedly rich world, connecting us to our deepest ınner resources".

"I wanted to find yet more ideas in the wind in order to wal better on this earth, as a doctor and as a human being".

hearts thumping in front of our nascent balloons. Part of us was no longer on earth but we weren't in the sky yet.

As I left the post office, where I'd gone to have my philatelic envelopes stamped, the five balloons before me were now fully inflated and perfectly lined up. It was hard to believe that they were for us, that we had been given the opportunity to live this adventure.

I was happy to share this moment with Richard, as I had a pretty good idea of how he felt. He had been on the lift-off site of *Double Eagle II* with his father. I could feel this race was made for the two of us. He was going to be reunited with his father over the Atlantic, and I would be reunited with my grandfather. We each had a family episode to live out and I sincerely hoped we would manage it. He looked very surprised when I tackled such a personal subject with him. He'd never got over the shock of his parents's death in a plane crash. Although he used to hide his pain behind a somewhat surly appearance, his straightforward handshake told you more about him than any discourse.

When I made my way to my capsule, I was far too excited to remain fully confident.

Then everything went very quickly. The Lord Mayor of Bangor gave us the keys to the city and gave the starting signal. Wim then cut off the strap which held us to the ground and we disappeared into the night.

For a while, a last tie still linked us to Bangor: a clear vision of Bass Park where the other four monsters were standing erect against the dark sky. We even saw Erich and Jochen's balloon lift off before they were swallowed into darkness. We suddenly felt as if we were part of a bubble detaching itself from the Earth and taking us to another world. We had often wondered how we would feel during the lift-off, and that particular moment suddenly justified the long wait in the USA. The impression was so strong that we felt totally lucid and aware of everything that took place, the black night into which we had disappeared, the first blasts of the burners, the first resounding message from the VHF radio, the limited size of our cabin, the mystery ahead of us…

It was almost daylight when we flew over the coast. It was now time to leave the continent and face the ocean. We had been waiting for this moment so eagerly, yet we were too worried and overworked to really enjoy it. Of course, we had learned the theory, but now we had to tackle the practice: GPS navigation, the reactions of the balloon, the means of communication. We slowly descended to sea level and flew over the last islands, our stomachs in knots, guessing that everything was going to be more difficult than we had originally thought. Several yachts and fishing boats escorted us to the sound of their foghorns. I think we crossed the coast near that little port where, three days earlier, we had lost all hopes of lifting off. The sun was rising and began to warm our envelope. We no longer needed the burners. The wind was pushing us towards the open sea in absolute silence and we felt drawn towards the horizon, over there, far away, towards the south-east: 3000 miles of water… We went past all the boats and were now looking behind us to cling a little bit longer to something familiar. We then heard some strange breathing noises coming from the ocean. Leaning overboard, we saw several whales and a multitude of dolphins in front of us. They all ignored us majestically, playing with nature, our only companion from then on.

An American voice on the radio reminded us once more:

'To Chrysler 1 from Boston Airport, you are now leaving American air space. Enjoy the flight and good luck!'

We were not heading towards Europe but South Africa! According to the Bangor weather forecast, the high altitude currents were closer to the north-east, and we let our balloon rise to the ceiling, relying only on solar warming. In fact, this course was not as good as when we were at sea level, we were now heading further south. But before we had time to correct anything, we heard a long ghastly creaking noise, followed by several other shorter ones. I felt my heart stop. As we looked above, we realised that the swelling of the envelope seemed to have stretched the seams of the appendix too much and the helium couldn't overflow freely. Did that mean the fabric was tearing apart due to the increased pressure of the gas? We didn't have much time to think about it as we were interrupted by a series of other dreadful creaks that sounded just like when you tear a rag apart. I was paralysed with fear, my throat felt tight. I looked at the ropes we would have to pull to turn the envelope into a parachute if the balloon exploded. We would have to be quick. I brusquely realised the difficulty, not to say the danger of this adventure. I felt ill and tired after the sleepless night of the lift-off and I reckon Wim had his heart in his boots too:

"Put your parachute on, and call Cameron on the VHF; I'll keep an eye on the envelope".

Later, Erich would tell me:

"A pity you couldn't hear your voice on the radio when you informed us that the balloon was being torn apart!"

Some 11,000 ft below there was nothing but icy water… and the opening of the capsule was so narrow that we couldn't both jump at the same time. Don couldn't understand the origin of these noises but he seemed to be confident in his manufacturing. Another crew had just called him to inform him about a similar phenomenon, but their balloon was still flying… It could be that some frost had obstructed the overflow. In which case, the pressure would either make the balloon burst, or it would unstick the overflow and re-establish the circulation. Fortunately, that seemed to be the case and, after several other terrifying creaks, we suddenly saw the tube dilate and the helium overflow before us. We'd had a narrow escape! But, despite our relief, we didn't feel like staying high up and we activated the valve many times to get back down to sea level: radio contacts between the teams had announced more favourable winds there. Indeed, when reaching 130 ft, we began to shift towards the north-east at 11 mph. That was very slow, but at least we were heading for the right direction. At that speed, we would need at least eleven and a half days to do the crossing, double our maximum range! And there was no way of going back.

Still shaken by the false alarm, we were now facing another problem: the solar radiation wasn't enough to maintain a stable flight level, and we had to use the burners as if there was a leak in the balloon. If that was the case, we would have to consider doing an emergency landing in Nova Scotia, which we were approaching. We looked at each other in dismay. So much effort for half a day's flight! What a let down! I even got to wonder if I wouldn't have preferred to wake up in Bangor and think it had all been a nightmare! We tried to keep the balloon at a height of 130 ft, but a strange mist lingering over the ocean prevented us from judging the distance. At some stage, the aerial of the HF radio was even touching the sea. We hadn't had anything to eat yet. Almost in a state of hypoglycaemia, I began to suffer optical illusions. Suddenly, I caught Wim by the arm and shouted at him:

"Look, there is a plane coming up below us, it's going to hit us". I froze on the spot and couldn't see how we might avoid the crash. It was only about 20 yards away. The roar also drew Wim's attention, but it wasn't an aeroplane! It was a fishing boat, and it wasn't coming up, we were going down into the mist. I felt stupid, but I also realised that exhaustion had greatly altered my powers of perception.

This first day was difficult, we were going from one scare to another, and I was beginning to wonder if I might not welcome a landing in Nova Scotia. We would be there around midday. In the meantime, the balloon began to behave more normally and we recovered our confidence. We decided to stake our all, to go ahead, even if we had to land on the sea later.

We were flying over dry land again, at an acceptable level, and although my stomach was unsettled, I forced myself to have a first meal: bread, tuna fish, cheese and nuts. Wim didn't eat anything and manned the vessel while I got a little sleep.

I had studied various investigations published in medical journals about sleeping in extreme conditions, that's to say when the night is interrupted by periods of activity. My conclusions were that the best moments to sleep were from 2 p.m. to 4 p.m. and 11 p.m. to 7 a.m., with a peak time between 3 a.m. and 5 a.m., whereas the worst moments, those which don't restore strength, were at the end of the morning and from 8 p.m. to 10 p.m.

If sleep had to be split into several periods, then small naps lasting 30 to 60 minutes were more profitable than those exceeding 1 hour.

Since we were two, I had planned two half nights and two afternoon naps, a good compromise which should allow us to have eight hours sleep each, split in two lots.

In fact, we never managed to apply this programme. Both of us were far too busy managing the flying and the navigation, but also too fascinated with what was happening. We couldn't waste our time sleeping! The understanding between us got to be so good that we would just compare the fatigue of the moment to decide on the sleeping turns. So, to the hell with the theory! Our only aim was to avoid being both exhausted at the same time.

Despite the sleepless night we'd spent inflating the balloon, Wim wasn't tired yet, so I was the first to use the berth. I'd always had a very light sleep, easily disturbed by light or noise, and I was afraid of getting overtired during this expedition. After all, Don Cameron had failed in his attempt at crossing the Atlantic in 1978 because his faculty of judgement was blurred by exhaustion. Since

I didn't normally take sleeping tablets, I was afraid of using them in a situation where I might need to be fully awake and watchful. I was more interested in hypnosis. The press and the public were clearly interested in this project, but I couldn't guarantee the success of the method. This first afternoon nap would be the test.

Abandoning, almost to my regret, the panorama offered by the flight over Nova Scotia, I returned to the capsule, lay down and tried to memorise the lessons: I closed my right hand, tightening my fist, strongly, more and more, the tension increased until it got unbearable; I released my muscles brusquely, rolling my eyes backwards, took a deep breath then breathed out at length. This produced immediate relaxation. Concentrating on the regularity and the depth of my breathing, I focused the sensations on my abdomen, preventing my brain from being distracted by what went on out there. In this state of relaxation, I centred my will on trying to have a rest before allowing myself to fall asleep. Nevertheless, I couldn't forget the noise of the radio. Although I felt as if my body had gone to sleep very quickly, my mind remained attentive to the messages which Wim was exchanging with the other crews. I had just discovered a state of conscious sleep that was new to me: my body was profoundly resting while my mind kept watchful.

I remained in this state for four hours. The heat was suffocating as the inner aluminium coating turned the capsule into a solar oven where the temperature could reach over 104°F. I felt as if I was roasting, and I wanted to know where we were. I then concentrated on breathing in and began to activate the muscles in my arms, letting my sensations get to the surface. My eyes opened onto a reddish sky which I could see through the opening of the capsule. The sun was setting on the horizon; the serenity of the moment contrasted with the frightful hours we had been through during the first part of the day. Wim was sitting on the edge of our cabin, his camera in hand, relaxed and smiling. The balloon was flying well, level, without any need for the burners, and there was no question of doing an emergency landing anymore. The cause of that problem would always remain a mystery.

The emotions of the day came back to us like a mixed feeling of anguish and impotence, inherent to any flight in a balloon. The wind, and the wind only, decided on our flight path, and we could only change our altitude to find a more favourable layer. We lifted off, the wind swept us away and we were irreversibly propelled into the unknown. Our state of mind couldn't change anything. As we became gradually aware of it, we began to look at things differently, standing back a bit more; within ourselves, what normally made us react automatically before a dangerous situation was giving way to something a lot deeper: a kind of faith, of acceptance of the events that unfolded before us.

We couldn't change the situation, but we could let the situation change us, shape us, mould us differently.

When looking at the reddening skyline, we were aware that the sun sets every night over the Atlantic, that the wind blows where it pleases, and that nobody had obliged us to get into that situation. It was up to us to follow nature's rhythm, not the other way round. If we had suffered during that first day, it was because we had tried to resist what lay before us, out of habit. Now, we felt it was time to enter into a new relationship with the unknown. From the moment that sunset cast a spell on us, we tried to make the most of our flight, to enjoy every moment, to truly live the adventure for which we had made so many sacrifices. We accepted the irreversible, inexorable nature of the wind that pushed us towards the open sea.

Despite general belief, adventure is not a conquest carried out head high and standard in hand. On the contrary, adventure involves dealing constantly with doubts and emotions. It then crossed my mind that true adventurers can only be humble humans. I looked at my Chinese talisman. It wasn't that easy to let 'the wind blow your way'.

The night was now surrounding us completely, and we had put our lights on. There was very little space to move inside: the equipment was squeezed between the two berths. Finding anything, even an ordinary object like a fork or a toothbrush could take a few minutes. Every meal, every change of clothes, even having a quick wash required a bit of practice. Nothing could be done without the help of the other pilot. One had to move his head back to let the other get his arms into his jumper. The former had to move to a corner of the cabin to let the latter put the bucket on the floor and use it as a toilet.

It was Wim's turn to sleep and I found myself alone in front of the red switch which lighted the burners. Even though I had learned to fly in preparation for this race, I still had no licence and had never piloted a balloon by night. Wim's trust totally reassured me, but I already knew that malicious gossip would say that he'd crossed the Atlantic with a 'passenger' on board. I couldn't afford to make a single mistake. The important thing was to find and maintain the best relation between speed and direction, by keeping the flight as horizontal as possible. Firing the burners for too long would cause the balloon to rise too much and lead us southward. The opposite wouldn't be enough to slow the descent and that would cause us to get too close to the sea. We were only 1600 ft above the water but had no visual contact with it because of the fog. I got so concentrated that I began to feel that nothing existed out there, that I was in a bubble and followed its movements through the liquid crystals of a screen. Whereas, in fact, I was linked to the outer world via eight satellites. What a contrast! When I got my head out of the narrow opening of the capsule, the sight was breathtaking: billions of stars and a rising moon silently joined the balloon above a mass of clouds which stuck to the ocean. I knew that the other pilots were feeling just as fascinated, that they were thinking exactly the same as me. Among the English crew, Don Cameron had gone to sleep and Rob Bayly wrote in his journal:

'I'd never seen so many stars in my life. There's no light contaminating the sky and my mind is floating as freely as a balloon. There must be some kind of life on at least one of the planets which gravitate around the thousands of suns which are before me.'

On *Chrysler 5,* Troy turned towards Richard and said:

'I think the word 'respect' was created for a scene like this: a starry night above the sea. It's absolutely marvellous.'

When you look at the sky from the Earth, you see isolated stars around the Milky Way, but here, in total darkness, the sky was just an immense Milky Way!

I felt like telling Michèle about it all, to share my joy with her, but also to reassure her. What a strange impression it must have been for her to be expecting our second child in a cosy apartment, while our balloon was drifting over the ocean! Feeling immensely grateful to her for her trust, I wrote a fax out with the computer and hoped the Immarsat satellite would do the rest.

Then I exchanged a few words with Richard, who was flying even lower than us, but also in good conditions.

The muffled atmosphere of that first night was magical. We continued our race bit by bit over the immense map of the Atlantic, and I already wished it would never end.

The hours went by, marked by the noise of the burners 4 times a minute. I managed to keep the flight level and smiled at myself for taking this piloting lesson alone, at night, in the middle of the ocean. Wim's trust gave me wings! But I started to feel sleepy as I took some notes; the figures on the instrument got gradually blurred. I woke him up and took his place, falling asleep straight away. It was now his turn to be alone under the celestial vault.

When I woke up, we were starting the second day of our flight, almost static over a sea of clouds. I tried to stabilise the balloon on the upper limit of the layer, so as to expose only the top of the envelope to solar warming. This way, we would avoid ascending but we wouldn't have to open the helium valve all the time. This is how I spent my first hours playing with clouds, allowing myself only a short break to eat something.

Then, paying heed to Richard and Troy, who had reached a better speed at a height of 10,000 ft, we let the balloon rise despite advice from base to always remain below 5,000 ft. We reached our ceiling at 11,000 ft and, for the first time since our departure, we had nothing to do but watch our fully dilated envelope move at 15 mph over a sea of clouds. Up until then, all our attention had been centred on doing navigational tasks, deciphering the route predictions, piloting with burners, communicating via the fax and the radio, with no time left for proper meals. But that afternoon was like a dream. The balloon was flying on its own, heading the right way, and here we were, stripped to the waist, at the 'balcony' (the narrow edge of the capsule padded with foam). Unfortunately, given the ambient temperature, fresh food was not so fresh. We had a disgusting lunch made of melted cheese on dry bread rolls topped with hard boiled egg, which we could never have swallowed in an ordinary situation. But here, cut off from the usual standards of comfort and routine, we took things as they came. Human beings have an extraordinary power of adaptation. We had only been flying for thirty-five hours and that was nothing compared with what we would endure later! Yet, we were already beginning to love this Nature in the raw all around us: air, water, clouds and light. This was more or less how I had always imagined the creation of the world.

When we speak of nature in daily life, we mean plants, trees, insects, animals, in short, all that lives and moves before us. We usually pay very little attention to the mineral kingdom. But here, in the middle of the Atlantic, Wim and I witnessed the continuous metamorphosis of the elements, engaged in playful activities to produce all possible shades and sounds. The shadow and the light, engaged in a turbulent love dance, appeased or roused the ocean, whose waves sometimes echoed up to 10,000 ft. The permanent game between air and water created, shaped and distorted the cloudy curls which rays of sunshine could then sculpt and paint as they pleased. Here, the elements were truly alive.

I would never have thought that a sea of clouds covering the whole landscape could be so varied. Of course, it could be that what we saw around the balloon was actually a projection of our inner landscape. In any case, that day went fast, too fast. Our camera, fixed at the end of a 20 ft pole, was the only thing that allowed us to freeze some of those magical moments.

By the end of the afternoon, the helium began to cool down and contract. The balloon descended slowly and regularly to the level of the sea, which appeared brusquely before us as we pierced the bottom of the cloud layer. Since our departure, we'd used up a 21-gallon propane cylinder, which we were about to throw overboard to lighten the weight of the balloon overnight. The designer had planned it all, cylinders would sink quickly to avoid causing damage to any boat passing by. A clean cut in the strap with a knife and our first aluminium container was off, swirling down into the evening light before making a big splash 1000 ft below. The point of impact soon disappeared, we were glad to see with our own eyes that we were really progressing towards Europe.

Meanwhile, the stronger wind announced at the beginning of the afternoon made itself felt at last, and the GPS gave us some excellent parameters. Wim was beaming in front of our dials: altitude: 1,000 ft, heading: 45° (i.e. north-east) speed: 34 mph. Each balloon received a fax from Chrysler's base with an extrapolation of the flight paths, and the conclusion was obvious: the higher we flew, the further south we turned, the lower we flew, the further back north we headed. This allowed us to choose our direction more freely by simply altering our altitude. At 3 o'clock in the morning, when Wim woke me up, the balloon was 1,000 ft above sea level and we were heading back much further north than the others and much faster too. We swapped places and Wim fell fast asleep. We would have to leave his initiation to hypnosis for another occasion…

I was now flying at a height of 1,650 ft and a speed of around 44 mph. The roaring sound of the waves reached us, confirming a change in the weather. This was no longer the glassy sea of the first two days. I was dying to see the sunrise over the ocean in all its splendour, but with the layer of clouds which covered us, all I could see was a faint grey light which didn't affect my concentration.

I felt like seeing what was going on a bit higher up at around 13,000 ft. The arrival through several layers of clouds was magnificent: we were side by side with the woolly peaks of enormous cumulus clouds. They were just next to us, truly alive, taking on one shape and another according to the masses of air heated by the sun. We played hide-and-seek with the shadow and the light, every firing of the burners allowing us to emerge, as if to recover our breath, before plunging again into the misty veil of the clouds. This fascinating game played by the elements will be one of the most memorable moments of our crossing.

That third day we were able to speak with our relatives. Telephone communications via satellite didn't exist yet, and our HF radio messages had to be commuted to normal telephone through the relaying of coastal stations, specialised in long distance communications with ships. This way, via Ostende Radio in Belgium and Berna Radio in Switzerland, we managed to have some very clear conversations with Europe. But we forgot about the technical part when Wim heard his mum's voice come out of the loudspeaker. He got hold of the microphone almost crushing it, his voice was trembling as much as his mother's and I shared their emotion in silence; during the past few weeks I had realised how deeply attached he was to her.

At that very instant, I missed my mother more than ever. I looked back on all the events that had been linked since I was a little boy for me to be where I was now, playing with clouds and radio waves at the height of adventure. First, my passion for rockets in Cape Kennedy, where Wernher von Braun and Charles Lindbergh had introduced me to the astronauts who were going to the Moon; then my first attempts at hang gliding which, from loops to drops, had led me to the world of aeronauts where I'd met Wim. How many pieces had to be cut by destiny to form the puzzle of one's existence… I also felt very grateful to my parents for always letting me develop an interest in every opportunity that presented itself, without ever conditioning my thoughts.

A few minutes later, during an interview, I heard Michèle's voice coming from a radio studio.

I bit my lip to try and contain my emotions. I felt a bit selfish to be risking my life and the future of my family to take part in an expedition like this, but I also knew that this flight would be tremendously enriching. I had the strange feeling that I'd had to embark on this adventure, that I hadn't really had any choice.

'Michèle, darling, I love you. Thanks for letting me go. Tell Estelle that her dad will be home soon.'

Well, so to speak: there was nothing we could do but follow the wind that was blowing our way…

How strange it was to exchange loving words which could be heard by hundreds of thousands of listeners! Then again, our whole flight was full of contrasts: our isolation and our dialogues with the whole world; our minute cabin and the immensity of the ocean; our worry and our absolute faith. After these few words, silence invaded our cabin again and we remained speechless for a long while, as if to savour a bit more the intensity of these moments.

In an attempt to try and immortalise the night which had now swallowed us, Wim fixed a flash on his camera, and, from the tip of our pole, the lightening pierced the shroud of darkness for a hundredth of a second. Then I resolved to go to bed and fell asleep after a session of self-hypnosis. I suggested to myself that the ambient noise wasn't going to bother me, but I would have been better off telling myself I wasn't going to hear anything at all. During the next hours, I experienced again this curious dissociation between my body which was asleep and my mind which paid attention to life in the capsule. In fact, I didn't have a single dream throughout those nights, probably because I was 'in' the dream.

Wim had little room to move about and pushed me inadvertently on several occasions. I must have been in some kind of sleep since I didn't react. I wasn't annoyed at him. I even felt a lot of affection for him, imagining him alone at the controls, under the rain which was now falling! Indeed, despite the reassuring faxes, it was now raining! I could even hear the drops fall on the Plexiglas dome and I perceived everything around me even before leaving my hypnotic state.

The wind had got a lot stronger and when I calculated our position I could hardly believe it: we had just taken the lead in the race! I wrote it down into my notebook, adding between brackets and with a big question mark: 'provisionally'? At the lift-off, the people of Bangor had placed their bets on us, but the favourites of all the specialists had been those who already knew the traps of the Atlantic: Don and Evert. We had nothing to lose, and now we suddenly felt that we were winning something. However, we were not going to let this trouble our serenity. Our aim was still to cross the Atlantic, and a victory should only be the icing on the cake. For a short while, I thought to myself:

"Now, we've proved our ability; at least we'll have been the leaders of the first transatlantic race for a while; whatever happens to us, people will remember us a just a little."

But such considerations weren't on my mind for very long. Every time I put my head out, I came face to face with the raging ocean. The roaring noise of the waves reached us, it sounded as if the sea wanted to project its foam right up to the sky. Several layers of threatening clouds surrounded us, blocking off the horizon as if to prevent us from escaping. I couldn't get it into my mind that we were there, in the middle of a storm, in a tiny balloon which tried to make its way across the fury of the elements. But there were still no signs of turbulence despite our 56 mph, since we were moving with the wind. The storm carried us, went with us, it may even have had no intention to harm us.

Yet, heavy from the rain, the German balloon was crawling along, level with the waves. The burners were not enough to keep it flying and the pilots were getting ready for an emergency landing. To our anxious questions, the race control centre replied from Rotterdam that it couldn't be raining since there weren't any clouds on the images received by satellite! This stupid statement was immediately refuted by Luc Trullemans from the Royal Institute of Meteorology in Brussels (RIM), now in contact with Wim: we were facing a depression likely to follow us all the way to Europe, unless we ascended as far as possible at once. Since in Rotterdam they gave us the order to fly as low as possible, we were caught up in their contradiction. However, I was inclined to trust the RIM which had advised my grandfather so wisely for his stratospheric ascents, and we decided to go upwards, at the risk of freezing the balloon.

We could still see the Atlantic churning between the clouds for a while, then we disappeared among a layer of nimbostratus, with the dreadful impression of being immobile and blinded all of a sudden. Only the figures and the needles on our dials seemed to be alive, like our burners which were spitting some blazing gas out. We held our breath, motionless under the closed dome, searching for the first sunrays through the grey shroud of rain which surrounded us. On several occasions, the light changed and we thought we'd gone through the layer, but it never ended: the rain hadn't stopped. If Luc had got it wrong, we wouldn't get near the sun before reaching our ceiling, and we'd have lost our bet. At this altitude, with a frozen balloon, the propane consumption would be enormous and we would be unlikely to reach Europe. We couldn't stay under the rain.

At this very moment, I remembered the synchronicities which preceded my departure, the obstacles which disappeared spontaneously, and the pressing feeling that I had to take part in this race. On one hand, I felt tiny in that situation about to turn into a disaster, on the other, I had total faith in that adventure. If all had gone well until now, it couldn't possibly end in a landing in the middle of the Atlantic at the height of a storm. There was no need to speak, Wim and I shared this feeling tacitly. We were both calm despite our anxiety and waited under the rain for the needle of the altimeter to continue progressing on the dial. Suddenly the rain turned into snow, but we continued with our ascent.

The needle indicated 13,000 ft when the sun pierced the clouds at last, revealing a magical scene: snowflakes scintillating under the sunbeams, an iridescent layer of clouds topping the sky, and long icicles hanging from all the ropes of the balloon. Our hearts beat faster, but we knew from the beginning of this adventure that it was dangerous to be taken over by euphoria. It seemed we had won our bet, but we continued ascending to get above the snowfall. The balloon stabilised itself at maximum height, 16,000 ft above sea level, next to the highest clouds. We were beginning to overtake the front. Our speed reached 53 mph under an icy sun, barely hot enough to dilate our helium and allow us to switch the burners off. We got the oxygen cannulas out and opened the breathing circuits.

We spent all day truly surfing the front of bad weather which stayed with us until evening, always visible to the north. Every time we let the balloon descend inadvertently, it would overtake us and darken the sky. We ended up playing with a threatening barrier of nimbostratus, which, far from stopping us, actually pushed us even faster towards Europe!

In the meantime, Richard, who had decided to ascend from the beginning of the rainfall, had reached his ceiling at around 16,500 ft and was being pushed towards Morocco. He didn't know then the significance this would have for him. His voice on the radio was totally calm, he piloted like a true professional, when in fact he was staking his family reputation with every firing of the burners.

For their part, Erich and Jochen had just landed in some 23 ft-deep trough and had been rescued by a tanker which, to cap it all, was heading for America. Wim and I were upset. Even though they were safe, it felt as if we had just lost two friends. The race would continue without them, without their friendly messages, and especially without them fulfilling our common dream: to cross the Atlantic.

We began to fear being caught up by the front of bad weather again, and we spent the rest of the day scrutinising the horizon. All the more so, since we had openly disobeyed the orders given by the official meteorologists of the race.

It was time to send news to our relatives and, from the loud-speaker of the radio, a voice reverberated among the interference: it was Laurent, Wim's young son. I took the video recorder to immortalise the moment. Wim took his sunglasses off as his eyes were misty with emotion. He spoke in Flemish, but in moments like that you get to understand any language.

Lulled by Laurent's little voice questioning his father, I leaned out of the capsule to look at the sunset and the reddish clouds. I experienced a mixed feeling of fear and fascination and told myself that we couldn't have a grudge against Nature for trying to swallow our two friends. It followed its course unperturbed, with or without them, with or without us, and, truly, it was man's fault if he threw himself into the lion's jaws.

And why indeed? Why did we go and explore the kingdom of the Elements with our terribly limited means? At this very moment, the reply was crystal clear. Why did we want to cross the ocean? Well, to experience this unbelievable feeling of communion with Nature, with technology, with ourselves and between us. We left our daily reality, our ordinary world, to get to the core of the myth of the eternal struggle between man and nature. But we now had to face the facts which clearly spoke for themselves: there was no more struggle, no fighting, but, on the contrary, a deep friendship, perhaps even love for all that surrounded us. There was no more contradiction between humanism and technology, between intuition and electronics, between man and nature, between the sky and the ocean. It all existed side by side and we needed it all. Prejudice didn't hold any longer on the threshold of the unknown, I suddenly felt I was being myself. I now saw my daily life and social conventions from so far above that I couldn't help but wonder why I usually gave so much importance to so many trivial details. I was being transported by the current of life which had been flowing for billions of years, well before beings got to the human stage. I felt fully alive, with such deep consciousness and sensitivity that I wanted to crystallise them in me for the rest of my life.

But, God, how difficult it was to put into words the vision which had just flashed past us! Leaving aside the official logbook for a while, I sat before the blank pages of my personal notebook. This was where I did my best to jot down my impressions and take some notes which would later allow me to experience these sensations again, and maybe even share them with someone. Extreme adventure, the real one, is not for showing off in public, nor is it an escape from reality or a wish, whether conscious or not, to get high on adrenaline. On the contrary, extreme adventure is what allows you, through emotions you wouldn't normally experience in daily life, to enter into a much more intimate relationship with your self. A more genuine one too, because you cannot cheat before the immensity that surrounds you. It is a life-size mirror, and the opportunity to discover some new inner resources.

Adventure is that breaking point when we realise that we can no longer be satisfied with reproducing automatically what we learned, that this won't do anymore. We then have to accept the doubts and the question marks, and even use them, to stimulate our creativity and be capable of producing behaviours, attitudes, strategies and solutions we have never learnt. It is a way of exploring the inner world more than the outer one, to draw from our deepest inner self what we have never learned to use so far. In a way, adventure is a crisis which we accept, which we even provoke at times, like this transatlantic race, whereas, on the contrary, a crisis is a possible adventure which we reject, for fear of losing control.

I am always surprised to see how we usually exploit only a tenth of our capacity of consciousness and sensitivity. How rich life would be if man accepted to open up to his true nature and to take a step off the beaten track! No, truly, adventure isn't something we do, it's something we live, something we feel, something we experience. It's a frame of mind open to the unknown.

We found ourselves in a contradictory situation. On one hand, we were entirely dependent on the wind that pushed us, almost prisoners of the weather forecast, and on the other, we felt totally free to be ourselves, as if suddenly liberated from the past or the future which usually condition us. We lived every second, enjoyed every moment to the full. We had the incredible sensation that time was stopping. Contemplating the ocean around us was no longer monotonous. Quite the opposite. In fact, we were beginning to see, a bit blurred and far away, a new way of perceiving life. We could have been proud to lead the first transatlantic race, we could even have pretended it didn't fascinate us, I could have imposed my medical views on Wim and he could have imposed his captain's orders on me, but in fact none of this happened. The wind pushed us, taking away our usual reflexes, our principles, and our usual behaviour before life's events. Having stood back helped us to feel nothing but tolerance and comprehension for all those who lived and thought differently. It suddenly didn't matter who was right and who was wrong, what was positive and what was negative, because all that happened on earth was in fact one of the numerous facets of life as a whole. What became important was the very fact of living, of feeling that we were all drinking from the same source, even if we drank differently.

Yet I knew full well that this extraordinary impression of communion was only possible through the artificial situation in which we found ourselves; our bubble had detached itself from the earth at Bangor and we would eventually get back to the everyday world. But that didn't sadden me, it was an integral part of the experience. The wind that blew would necessarily take us back to daily life. But, it may not be quite the same as before now that we had come into close contact with the ocean and with ourselves in a privileged way for a few days. Life had acquired a different flavour which would probably encourage us to continue along that path. Indeed, everything we now felt could only be a foretaste of true adventure: learning to open up to a rich inner life. With normal daily routine, the path is obstructed by a mass of prejudices and irrational fears which prevent us from questioning ourselves. Whilst there, between the sea and the sky, between America and Europe, between uncertainty and mystery, the unknown became an ally.

Not knowing at any time what the future had in store for us, having to guard against all eventualities, Wim and I had to keep our hearts and minds open. Open to the unforeseen, to the storm, to the burners breaking down or the valve not working, to a sea landing, to success or failure. This state of total open-mindedness kept us lucid, watchful and centred. We were amazed to see that we had become much more efficient than in ordinary life. Although it usually frightens people, the unknown can truly be an ally and may even become a friend.

All these ideas were merely thoughts of mine on that fourth evening and I still did not know how the adventure would end. For all I knew, my notes might get drenched under the threatening sky. In fact, the news was bad. *Chrysler 4* had been caught up by the rain and Evert would later say:

'It was really difficult; we were advised to fly low and we were 165 ft above the sea, only 165 ft, in total darkness, under the rain and in the bad weather, but going at an excellent speed. It was frightful. Every time we opened the porthole, we could hear the sound of the storm, as if the ocean was saying, "Hey, little balloon, come here, I'm going to swallow you!" The envelope was getting heavier and heavier, and Gerhard was constantly struggling to remain at that level. Then, the rainfall died down and we managed to reach a sunny spell higher up. This was when we realised that we were catching up with the Belgian balloon, so we decided to keep quiet on the radio to create a surprise.'

Meanwhile, Wim said goodbye to Laurent, and Ostende Radio put me in touch with Michèle. I had so many things to tell her; yet everything I said seemed totally trivial. I would have liked her to share my experience but I think that as far as emotions were concerned she'd already had her share, especially now that they kept on mentioning on the news how many times the crossing of the Atlantic had ended up in a disaster!

The sun had now disappeared behind the barrier of nimbostratus and Wim laid down to try and get some sleep. The radio and the fax printer didn't leave us in peace. We continued being approached by the European media, and every time we received the weather forecast we got all excited. Wim kept on turning over and over again on the narrow bunk and couldn't get to sleep. In the end, he asked me to help him with hypnosis.

Whether it was because of the coffee we had prepared on the small camping gas, or the continuous noise of the instruments, or simply because we logically felt tense at the thought of being so close to the goal, there was no way we could afford to lose some sleep. We were not in a cosy psychiatrist's practice but hanging from a ball of helium in the middle of the ocean, and I didn't know if it was going to work. I had to try and be confident that it wouldn't fail. I could see myself again at the seminar on hypnosis a few months earlier and became fully concentrated:

"Wim, you could fix a point, the middle of your thumb, for example… stretch it above the skyline… there we are… that's fine. Your arm is stretched… and it may become a little heavier… perhaps a lot heavier… like your eyelids… which will eventually close by themselves…"

I only spoke while he breathed out, adapting my breathing pattern to his. Every fifteen seconds, I would fire the burner to warm up our helium as the night was now icy.

"That noise you can hear is all right… I'm the one who's piloting… you don't have to do anything… your breathing is getting heavier… like your arms… and your eyelids… here we are. The arm can fall down now… like this… that's fine…"

Wim was now lying on his back, with his eyes closed, his face relaxed.

"I'm the one who's piloting; you can imagine that the balloon is moving away on its own… you don't have to do anything at all".

After the relaxing stage, I had to lead him to dissociation, in other words, I had to suggest that he wasn't in the balloon anymore and therefore didn't have to worry about it. Feeling liberated, he would then be able to sleep.

"Imagine that you can see the balloon drifting away and passing a rainbow… all is well, all is going softly. The white envelope begins to blend into the colours of the rainbow… you can see it go across the red band, red like the excitement which is about to disappear completely. Then the balloon crosses the orange band… and the yellow one… it becomes even calmer. The green band welcomes it… green, like the huge fields where all is so quiet. At the end of the fields, the balloon disappears slowly into the blue band… the sky is getting a little colder, a little heavier, a little darker. The rainbow turns to purple, the balloon is at a standstill and disappears. Everything has stopped for you and you may sleep happily, as much as you like since I'm the one who's piloting the balloon. Now everything has gone beyond the purple band, into the dark night… where you are asleep".

For me, this was also the moment of truth. I was afraid he might lift his head and ask: 'Is that it?'! He turned to one side and I checked whether he was opening his eyes, but he wasn't. A deep sigh indicated that he was already fast asleep. I was as happy as a child who's just managed to complete his first puzzle. Wim was now calm and relaxed in the safe world I had suggested to him, but I wasn't! The billions of stars shining around me were not enough to make me forget that another front of rain could be on the way. I watched the horizon, from north-west to north-east to find some stars, but I couldn't. The clouds were hidden in the night, yet I could feel their presence.

Now the temperature had gone down to −8°F. I tried to close the porthole, but the aluminium coating on the walls condensed the humidity, which began to run down around me. It would have to stay open. The biting cold was vivifying, I even leaned outside, as if to let the night seize me. The stars seemed even brighter, all danger had gone and I suddenly felt like melting into the starry sky. It was half past midnight when the Moon rose, revealing a completely clear ocean below. Not a cloud to disturb the reflection of the Atlantic, which seemed to leave the route to Spain wide open for us.

A thought crossed my mind: I was pursuing in a balloon the Gulf Stream route which my father had explored in a submarine twenty-three years earlier. Leaving from Florida with a crew of six scientists to let himself drift along this famous warm current off the coast of the USA, he had resurfaced a month later in the open sea off Nova Scotia. But the Gulf Stream didn't stop there. I could still hear my father tell me that, in theory, it was possible to pursue the drifting-and-diving across the Atlantic all the way to England then Spain. In fact, I was taking over his expedition. I was too young at the time to understand what he must have gone through during those thirty days of scientific adventure, but I couldn't forget his beaming face when he watched the jets of water spouting from the fire boats celebrating the return of the mesoscaphe in New York Bay. He had gathered an impressive amount of oceanographical, biological and chemical data, but probably also a wealth of emotions, which I was now able to perceive.

My father had given me the key to success on board: you mustn't try to have the last word when a conversation gets somewhat tricky; it's best to let the tension drop by itself. This allows the protagonists to realise spontaneously, without frustration or touchiness, that some advice or a decision may have to be adjusted. During our psychological preparation at Bangor, Wim and I had spoken about that and I felt that I had received the legacy of the Gulf Stream adventure on that score too.

All human beings are bound to be the product of all they have gone through so far, and it would be useless to expect them not to react according to the habits life has given them. Depending on the situation, any crew is likely to be faced with differences of opinion. Denying this obvious fact, as is too often the case with human relations, is like denying the other party the right to be different. Above all, in practical terms, it is certainly a cause for disappointment, if not resentment. Indeed, if you expect a certain type of behaviour from your partners, if you project your expectations on them, reality can only be disappointing. On the contrary, the mutual acceptance of divergences opens the way to dialogue. This seems so obvious that I wonder what's the point of writing it down; and yet, it explains many relational problems.

I had been able to participate in my father's expedition, and had felt especially proud to paint a small portion of the submarine's hull, but I hadn't been able to witness my grandfather's stratospheric ascents. Besides, I was far too young for him to tell me, during the last years of his life, what he had really experienced in his tiny pressurised capsule. All the stories I'd heard later were tinged with the extraordinary consequences of this first flight to space. Hergé had only acted as the spokesman of public opinion when comparing the impact of his stratospheric flights to the first steps on the Moon. I knew this full well, having heard it so many times. But, as to the emotion my grandfather must have felt when being the first man to see the curvature of the earth, that incredible sensation of suddenly becoming a part of space, of not completely belonging to our planet anymore, of not knowing which part of the world he was going to return to, that I didn't know at all. When listening to recordings, I was stunned by the absence of emotion in his speech. All his descriptions were rigorous, and always very technical, but there was no way you could guess, between the words, what he had felt. For example, like after the incident with the first lift-off to the stratosphere, when the cord of the valve which makes the balloon come downwards had got twisted, then broken. A journalist had tried to make him admit that he had been frightened at the thought of being propelled at an altitude of 53,000 ft in less than thirty minutes without being able to pilot his balloon:

"Why be afraid? Throughout the history of aeronautics, there hasn't been a single case of a balloon not coming down!"

That's the image I kept of my grandfather: not of a mere human being but a scientist, almost an 'inventing' machine. That image stuck in my mind until the lift-off at Bangor, until that first night into which our balloon melted, until I felt sure that he couldn't possibly have been caught up only by his calculations. He must have experienced something else, some sensations which he never related. He may even have been afraid of mentioning them, but I suddenly discovered them, as he must have done. Almost motionless under the celestial vault, hanging from my lucky star, half-way between two worlds, the generation gap was getting narrower. Before starting the transatlantic race, I had received an encouraging letter from a friend saying:

"Maybe you'll be able to have a chat with your grandfather when you're up there".

I definitely felt very close to him now and I understood what he must have felt. Here I was, watching the same stars as him, from the capsule of a balloon which was carrying me, as he had been, through a mass of simple, human emotions.

Up until now, I'd always remembered my fabulous childhood with much nostalgia. For years I'd been absorbed by the adventures and experiences of my relatives. Once I had chosen to take up a career in medicine, people kept on asking why I hadn't followed in my father's and my grandfather's foot steps. I was deeply convinced that my choice suited me best, but it was sometimes difficult to accept the consequences. To think that Wim had chosen me as his team mate precisely because I was a doctor! And that it had reunited me with the family tradition…

This was the first time I didn't feel torn between two concepts; quite the opposite. All of a sudden, it seemed that I could reconcile myself with everything: my relatives' career and my own, aeronautics and medicine, science and the wind. It was a bit as if I was paying a debt to my lineage in order to be my true self at last.

I turned towards Wim, he was still sleeping peacefully. A Belgian man and a Swiss man in the same balloon, going through the same adventure, again. I felt a lot of affection for this man who had trusted me to help him. If it was destiny that had brought us together, it had also created a new friendship and I felt deeply happy about it.

I also felt utterly alive. Every sensation was being recorded in my memory, in my body, for ever. I knew already that it would be impossible to forget the flavour of the night, the cold biting my face, the strokes of the Moon over the Atlantic, all that alchemical mixture of sensations which made the moment last forever and where the feeling of existing lay entirely within the force of the wind.

We were being pushed towards the east, which the sunrise would soon set ablaze. But I wasn't sure I could hold on another four or five hours to witness it. Exhaustion tended to make me miscalculate the best course for navigation. After hesitating for a long while, I decided it would be wiser to wake Wim up and take his place.

"Wim, your breathing is getting lighter, more superficial; the balloon is coming back towards you and you are going back on board. You can now wake up and take over".

After stretching a little, he asked:

"Bertrand, why did you let me sleep for so long? It feels like a whole night has passed".

The experience had been fully satisfactory. Wim had slept for two hours under hypnosis and he felt as rested as if he'd had a whole night's sleep. He then took over, attending to the burners first, then observing the sunrise. He told me later that it had been one of the most beautiful ones he'd ever watched.

When I woke up after a few hours of self-hypnosis, the sight before us dissipated all remaining desire to compete: the light was blinding and the black shadow of the small rain clouds stood out over the shimmery ocean. All the clouds were below us, against such a clear background that the air and the water seemed to be inverted, the sky below and the Atlantic above. And beyond, still far away but almost within reach, a cloudy barrier probably indicated the beginning of the continent! 250 miles ahead of us, the first thermals off the Portuguese coast were turning into condensation. It was both greatly reassuring to feel we were arriving, and jolly frustrating not to approach the goal faster. That line of clouds seemed to be the same distance away all day, like a painting you can never reach. It worsened as we advanced more slowly. At midday, our speed had decreased to 25 mph and we suddenly discovered that the Dutch were catching up with us from the north at a speed of 75 mph.

How secretive! Whilst keeping almost silent with the other balloons over the radio, they had taken the risk to go up in a northwards direction again, crossing our path that went down southwards. Having had no news from them, we'd asked the base to give us their position, and were stunned when we read the fax. What an incredible turnaround in the situation! Only a few hours before, we were worried about them, and now they were about to overtake us. At that speed, they were likely to reach northern Spain just before us. On one hand, it seemed terribly upsetting to be nosed out and lose at the last minute all the advantage we'd gained in four days; on the other, we weren't going to let this change our attitude or our strategy, no way. We had deliberately chosen not to go back up in a northwards direction because of the violent winds which had been announced over the British Isles. The thought of losing the race wouldn't change that. The panorama that stretched before our eyes over thousands of square miles wouldn't make us forget our first goal: to reach the European continent, whether we arrived first or last, as long as we got there alive and with our feet dry. *Chrysler 4* might win, but there was no way we were going to risk spoiling what seemed the most beautiful day of our life going downwards again, just to cut in front of them.

The Americans had drifted away far south, but only a minute gap now separated us from the Dutch in this incredible finish. They reached our height again and headed towards the upper tip of Spain at double our speed. At the race control centre in Rotterdam, all the organisers and journalists held their breath but the ambient agitation and suspense strangely contrasted with the absolute calm which reigned over our balloon. At an altitude of 16,500 ft or more, we watched the events unreel like a film; we no longer felt part of the race, we were like onlookers. Of course, we wanted to win, in fact we were very keen on it, but we could see that the victory didn't depend on us. In a last act of faith, we had to let the wind and the elements take over. We would let them be and just follow along, no matter how impatient we were to reach that motionless coast, no matter how worried we were in case we didn't make it.

Wim and I were both leaning on the 'balcony', trying to fix once more in our memory all the details of that imposing panorama. Every cloud became a thought, every reflection a feeling, every shade of colour an emotion, and the sun setting over the Atlantic gave us thousands of them, as a last farewell gift. The feeling of altitude and lightness, the total well-being, the joy of being an integral part of all that surrounded us transformed the flow of time. Up until now, we had watched the sun rise over Europe; and that evening, as if for the first time, it would set over America, where we had come from. Bangor was now 'on the other side'.

Europe was there, in front of us, almost within reach, but now the night prevented us from keeping an eye on our progression.

When the printer rattled, we immediately thought that it was to inform us of Evert and Gerhard's victory. After all, this adventure would never have taken place without Evert Louwman. It would be a consecration after his failure in 1985.

In fact, it was the RIM telling us that the Dutch balloon was drifting in distress in the Bay of Biscay where it had been dragged by a storm. Its pilots were about to ditch in the sea and had just sent a distress signal. Poor Evert, he didn't deserve that.

We put our heads out of the porthole, searching the night for the umpteenth time, and came face to face with a barrier of light about 60 miles long. The lighting of the coast, from Vigo to Porto, stood out in the dark. We could see our goal for the first time and began trembling with excitement. We grabbed each other by the arms then, without a word, we contemplated these lights with increasing anguish as we didn't seem to be moving towards them. The VHF was mobilised for contacts with the Lisbon and Madrid airports whose approach routes we were cutting, whilst the HF was permanently plugged on Ostende Radio which passed us one call after the other. Wim and I, leaning overboard, waited for the moment when we would be flying over the first city lights.

Right, this was it! We were exactly above Viana do Castelo, this was exactly the moment we had waited for so long. We couldn't quite believe it was true, but in the end we reached the mirage.

We thought we would fall into each other's arms in tears, but, almost to our surprise we didn't. It should have been the most beautiful moment of the race, but it was only the end of the epic. As if paralysed, we watched the streets of that little port go by slowly below our capsule, without feeling the emotional release we had expected. Five months of preparation, five weeks of waiting and five days of total concentration ended up in that instant. We had won the first transatlantic race, but history was now behind us. We had to land and leave the dream against our wishes. We both felt immense joy and at the same time a certain sadness. All the images got mixed up before that dark sky adorned with Portuguese lights.

When daylight came back, we were deep in the Spanish mountains. The sun tried to make its way through the bad weather which had caught up with us, and the colours of that cold light were a little daunting. A light mist stagnated at the bottom of the valley but the shape of the clouds spoke clearly: high up the wind was very strong. Nature seemed to make an effort to contain itself a while more before exploding. We'd been debating until then whether or not we ought to shorten our flight, but the panorama now left no room for hesitation. With a heavy heart, I got hold of the burners to pilot one more time this balloon which had carried us so faithfully over the ocean. I still needed this kind of physical contact with it. Firing the gas little by little, I let it descend into the valley to try and shift our path southwards and escape being drawn towards the mountains, where we wouldn't be able to land. For a while, we went along a motorway and a high-voltage line. The noise and the speed of cars startled us as if we were from another planet.

Wim then chose a field near a village and accentuated the descent. As we braked a bit too hard during the last few yards, we felt the balloon rise again, and missed the landing. Obviously, it wasn't any keener on landing than we were! We waited to fly over the next village to have another go. That next attempt was fine: after touching the ground delicately at the bottom of a small basin, the balloon stopped in the scrubland.

127

I had no desire to abandon the capsule, neither did Wim. We knew that the first to leave the balloon would be the first to come out of the dream! We were going to find the world as we had left it, but we had changed an awful lot.

The storm was already rising. A violent wind gushed into the envelope and shook it in all directions, as if in a last sign of protest. Agonising, its rip panel wide open, *Chrysler 1* was empty and shuddered for the last few times. On the ground, a bag of ballast had fallen and already the American sand was blending into the Spanish earth. Half a millennium after the discovery of the New World.

We still had the whispers of the ocean in our ears, the shimmer of the Atlantic in our eyes when we arrived at the Geneva airport like heroes. The headings in the newspapers read: 'Victory over the Atlantic', 'Piccard and Verstraeten tame the ocean', 'A Belgian-Swiss triumph'. Wim and I looked at each other feeling a little awkward. We didn't feel we had vanquished, let alone tamed anything whatsoever. An intimate contact with the ocean had developed during our 3000-mile flight. We had spent five days and five nights trying to tame it; we saw it fall asleep under the reddish rays of the sun, we saw it waken and even fly into a rage. Its winds beating the waves and its clouds spewing their anger out. And on the last day, while we were about 18,000 ft high and nature was calm below, it had opened up before Europe. No, we hadn't vanquished anything at all; all we had done was accept to be carried, and, if the Atlantic eventually let us through, it was because we had become its friends. Modesty and gratefulness compelled us to specify this, just like our desire to break away from the image of man wanting to dominate nature.

At first, I wanted to live among these images and impressions which had enriched me so much. I didn't want to see the memories of that flight fade away. I didn't want to think that the adventure was over, that I would have to resume the normal course of my life.

"The only time when I can change anything in my life is neither in the past nor in the future – it is in the present moment".

"Consciousness cannot be acquired once for all, it has to be rediscovered again and again".

"I feel therefore I am".

"Life is strewn with signs and messages that testify of the existence of a world which is beyond us".

"Paradoxically, it is in the moments that we want to flee that the main keys to the answers are to be found".

"From up there, I may be able to have a chat with my grandfather".

But my life would never resume a normal course. I had learned far too many things to be the same as before. When going back to my job as a psychiatrist, I felt that my whole approach to life and medicine had changed. It was disconcerting, I found myself out of step with my own knowledge, my own conceptions and habits. Little by little, it dawned on me that the real adventure hadn't begun with the lift-off at Bangor but with the landing in Spain. No, the adventure wasn't over, quite the opposite: it had just begun!

I became aware of it through the lectures and interviews that followed. The more I spoke about it the more this transatlantic flight became an image of life itself. I don't mean life as we normally live it but as we could be living it. At the end of each lecture, I had the impression that even if I hadn't crossed the Atlantic, even if I hadn't projected computer-made images on the screen, I wouldn't have been lying when telling my story.

What I had brought back from the Chrysler Challenge applied as much to life in general as to any balloon race: the certitude that our deep-rooted fear of the unknown was what caused most of our suffering and that our lack of faith and intuition made us want to control existence instead of accepting the opportunities that came our way.

In our society, we are taught at an early age to be afraid of what we don't know, to avoid uncertainties, to banish doubt. The unknown is so frightening to us that we do our best to find, if not invent, certainties. We are encouraged to find the answer to every question, to substitute question marks for exclamation ones. We end up being satisfied with partial explanations, truncated knowledge, to the point of not seeing that some of our certainties are in fact mere prejudice. But how reassuring! People say that nature hates emptiness but that's wrong. Human beings are the ones who hate emptiness, and who insist on filling the gaps with explanations. We forget that questioning signifies opening our heart and our mind, whereas an exclamation mark is an end in itself. To appease our fears before life's uncertainties, we gradually stick in a rut and our habits are like blinkers that prevent us from seeing the mysteries around us. Without realising it, we then pay a very high price for this illusory safety; as we ignore the opportunities life gives us we regularly miss the chances to evolve.

Genuine adventure, as I'd discovered it, consisted in breaking away from this rigid mould. It wasn't a question of doing something spectacular but of living something 'extraordinary', in other words, something which removed us from the paralysing routine of ordinary life. But adventure entailed following the journey till the end, come what may, without the opportunity to change our mind half way through and refuse the experience. When the wind was carrying us towards the ocean, before 3,000 miles of open sea, we had no means of turning back. We were destabilised by the unpredictability of every situation, by the lack of landmarks. We were going through a painful breaking point as we sensed the danger we were facing. We could no longer apply our usual pattern of thoughts or our reflexes to our relationship, our life on board or our way of piloting. We didn't even know what the next minute was going to be like, but we had to continue.

After spending the first day trying to resist, we began to devise another way of functioning. Curiously, it was uncertainty that made us focus on the present and keep our minds open to any eventuality. We then became more successful and efficient because we were without prejudice and ready to adapt to a new situation. Paradoxically, the trust we had placed in the unknown increased our feeling of freedom.

However, aerial escapades have no monopoly in this field. There are hundreds of examples of situations which gain from this phenomenon. The artistic process is an example that speaks for itself. A painter or a musician who sets to work intending to apply only the knowledge acquired at art school or at the conservatory will produce a good adaptation of all that already exists. But, before a white canvas or a blank score, if they truly follow their intuition they will produce a real masterpiece. The principle of hypnosis, or even meditation, is just the same. It is a way of temporarily breaking off from the ordinary world to enter into a relationship with inner or outer creative forces, and that's also an adventure. If you extrapolate a little, our entire life could become an extraordinary adventure if we managed to take advantage of the opportunities to break the mould and use them to stimulate our creative potential. Such situations, those moments when we lose control, often come our way but we do everything we can to avoid them because they look like times of crisis or drama. Accidents, bereavement, divorce, illness, retirement or unemployment painfully oblige us to modify our way of thinking and living our daily life. They are irreversible events, and our only freedom of manoeuvre consists in choosing the attitude we will adopt to face them. We may regard them as absurd and refuse to accept them, or we may see them as an inevitable opportunity to search for new resources within ourselves to cope with the situation and evolve. In short, no matter how painful they might be, these storms which sometimes disturb our peace are perhaps not all meant to swallow us up. On the contrary, they may encourage us to develop our creative strength against destiny, forcing us to a certain aloofness, a reappraisal of our values, even a certain independence or an increased responsibility towards ourselves.

But to perceive that, you have to begin having as much faith in the course of life as you would in the wind blowing over the Atlantic. The task is not easy. Some events can be tremendously violent and painful. This is something I had wanted to study and it was the theme of my doctoral thesis.

In *Learning from your ordeals*, I carried out an investigation on the positive effects which illness, accidents or misfortune may have on human personality. Strangely enough, most people I interviewed told me that after going through an ordeal they'd opened their mind to other dimensions, of a religious, philosophical or spiritual nature; they'd felt stronger after acquiring this new faith in the essence of life, this new intuition. But first of all, they'd had to find themselves at the heart of the suffering before they could accept the inevitable without rebellion and open up to something else.

I hope the reader will not misunderstand me or get the wrong impression at this stage. I'm not recommending the sort of fatalism that consists in blissfully accepting all that happens to us. To be fatalistic means not to try and change what we can change, not to struggle when we ought to. We can't always behave as if we piloted a balloon and depended on the wind. At times, we have to behave as if we were piloting a fighter plane. There are a great number of problems in life against which we can and must react. In my thesis, I tried to study the catastrophes of life, which occur irreversibly. The more you refuse to accept them, the deeper the suffering; the more you refuse to give your life a new direction, the more anxious you get.

Indeed, to avoid fatalism we often fall into the opposite excess, stress. Stress is usually regarded as the opposite of serenity, when for me it is only the opposite of fatalism. Stress consists in wanting to control or change what cannot be controlled or changed. In other words, in trying to act like a fighter pilot in a situation where it would be more useful to know how to fly a balloon!...

Life as such is not easy, but it becomes even more difficult if you can't accept it. I have always been moved by patients who arrive at my practice and say: 'my life is changing but I don't want to change; I've lost what I loved, please help me to be as I was before'! In most cases, that's impossible. The patient clings desperately to what he doesn't want to give up, to his fear of the unknown, his rejection of a different life and he suffers all the more for it.

The therapy then consists in helping the patient to progressively accept his potential to change, to question things; it is up to him to discover during the sessions that his whole life may be perceived like a big adventure, in which crises and misfortune as much as hopes and success inevitably force us to have a different relationship with the unknown. This is the only way we can evolve, assuming of course that we believe human beings are worthy of evolving. If we consider that man comes from nothingness, that he isn't going anywhere and that the purpose of life is only to bear as best we can the passing of time, from a useless birth to an inexplicable death, then my writings don't mean a thing.

My eighteen years of flying into the wind with the hang glider had definitely given me an inkling of all this, but I'd had to learn flying with the wind for it to become practical and useful in my research. I had thought that the only way to be efficient was to control everything in the present moment and against the wind. Now I knew that losing control permitted a much higher performance, more self-awareness, in life, that would be even more durable. I felt as if I'd learned more in five days than in several years of study, and this time my job as a psychiatrist wasn't out of step with my activities in the air. Nevertheless, I could no longer favour Jonathan Livingston's recommendation of 'wanting to be'. I had replaced aerobatics with a lecture tour called *'Adventure is a state of mind'* and I always finished with one of the Beatles's song which Joan Baez sang so beautifully: *Let it be.* Let our sensitivity, our emotions, our intuition of what is Essential, our trust in the breath of Life, let it all be.

A beautiful allegory of the 'let it be' concept had been shown to me by Richard Abruzzo at the end of the Chrysler Challenge. When Wim and I had landed and the English were collecting their equipment from the Portuguese beach which they had finally reached, Richard was still flying in the American balloon. Up until then, his father's balloon had held the record of the longest flight in history, but as we did our calculations we suddenly realised that *Chrysler 5* had flown longer than *Double Eagle II*, longer than any other balloon in the past. But this absolute record of duration was even more meaningful to Richard, who took it as a gift from his father. The duration record would remain within the family. I learned later that, for the first time in a long while, Richard had allowed himself to cry as a flow of released memories had suddenly filled his heart; the very memories he had kept buried in a dark corner of his mind to avoid suffering, since his parents had died in that tragic plane crash in 1985.

To think that throughout the last day of the flight, the race meteorologists had informed him by fax that he wouldn't get anywhere and that he had better ditch in the sea at once! Richard and Troy certainly saw themselves drifting towards Africa, but why land if the flight could go on? In the end, they arrived in Morocco and after 144 hours of flight they were able to reflect on how incredibly lucky they had been to manage this world record which was so symbolic for Richard.

The reflexes of everyday life prompt us too often to struggle in order to get what we want, without really knowing whether or not it's going to be beneficial to us. The way we usually look at problems is too narrow, too partial for us to get a global vision. In this respect, Richard and Troy could have struggled to reached the goal which had been set beforehand, to reach Europe, without knowing that this would deprive of from the world record. If they had faced the storm, instead of avoiding it by ascending immediately to 16,500 ft, they would certainly have reached Portugal, but they would only have come second or third. Then, the storm which forced us to land would also have prevented them from going ahead and they would have been a few hours away from the record of duration! By accepting things as they were, rather than trying to dominate them, they had been carried by the wind towards an even greater success than the one they'd imagined. I later came across this thought by the Dalai Lama:

'Not getting what you want is sometimes a marvellous stroke of luck…'

The flight in a balloon had taught me much about life, maybe more than all I had learned so far, but I still wanted to learn more. It was no longer a question of sport. It had become a way of life, a philosophy by which we go along with the events we cannot change, to use them to our advantage. I wanted to continue following that trace in the sky, which was beginning to leave a permanent mark in my heart. I wanted to find yet more ideas in the wind to continue walking with my feet on the ground, as a doctor and as a human being. This is why I embarked on a project which had been regarded as impossible so far, a project which would allow me to play with the unknown, with Nature, and to explore the inner world as well the outer one: going round the earth in a balloon, without an engine or a rudder.

THE LONGEST FLIGHT

The wonderful mystery of a question with no answer

THE IMPETUS WAS BROKEN, THE DREAM SHATTERED. The waves hitting the sides of the capsule finished dismantling the solar panels. Partly ripped open, the immense silver envelope was floating between currents. A large twin-engine plane from the French Navy was flying 70 ft above us, flapping its wings to guide the rescue boat. Wim and I, in our survival suits, helmets on, strapped in life-jackets, shyly lifted our arms every time the plane passed over what was left of our sumptuous balloon. Several similar attempts, made by American and Englishmen, had already failed after less than a day's flight and I had felt really sorry for the pilots. But this time, it was happening to us. We were racked with a painful feeling of shame about this awful waste. So many people had placed their trust in us, taking part in the preparation of this journey round the world, and here we were, paddling in the Mediterranean, hardly six hours after lifting off like heroes. This increased my sadness even more.

The extraordinary memories of the launch were blurred by the tears we could barely hold back. Throughout the night, our monster had stood erect in the icy sky over Château-d'Œx, among the liquid helium vapours made iridescent by the spotlights. Thousands of human shapes had been strolling like ghosts to see the magic show, which a hundred specialists or more had been orchestrating for the past twenty-four hours. When Wim and I had climbed into our yellow kevlar capsule, bristling with aerials and filled to the brim with provisions and fuel, the crowd had hailed us as if we'd already won our bet. We had drawn on our courage and found the strength to leave our respective families. Even before the balloon had lifted off, our hearts were already airborne. We had to concentrate to survive these two weeks in jet streams.

A few minutes after a majestic departure greeted by all the bells in the village, heavy with our dreams and the hopes of a huge crowd of spectators, *Breitling Orbiter* had reached the fiery glow of sunrise. Escorted by a cloud of helicopters, it had then acquired the brightness of a thousand suns. After four years of preparations, we had lifted off at last. We had embarked on what the media called 'the last big planetary adventure', in one of the most beautiful balloons ever built, and we'd barely covered 300 miles.

We had disappointed so many people. Adults and children alike had been thrilled and had given us signs or words of encouragement; our dream had become theirs. Some twenty different countries had written to us, through their national Olympic committee, to thank us for dedicating this flight to the protection of our planet. Part of my farewell speech still resounded in my head, like one more wound:

"We want to fly over the earth because it is beautiful. Our world could also be beautiful, if only human beings tried to dream a lot more. Without dreams, without elevation, without altitude, without standing back from our problems, we just stagnate in the quagmire of life, we're paralysed. While we're going through this adventure, remember that life in itself is an extraordinary adventure. It is a quest for guidance, to enable us to get closer to Nature, to better fulfil our role as a nexus between the sky and the earth, to project more love and shed more light around us".

How painful it was to see the remains of our dream scattered by the swell 20 miles off the French coast. It was the biggest failure of my life, and with all that media coverage nobody could ignore it! Somehow, this was a way of being immunised, we could never feel more ridiculous in the future! It was also a way of discovering that the pioneering spirit isn't automatically associated with great achievements. A pioneering spirit means above all accepting the risk of failing, accepting the risk of seeing the whole world laugh at you, and start all over again, despite of it all.

The next day, we answered questions from the press with puffy eyes. If you agree to speak to journalists when all goes well, you have to take it upon yourself to do so when things go wrong.

"Yes, there was a massive kerosene leak on board. The flange of a tube gave way during the ascent, because of a difference in the pressure. One of the tanks was spewing its contents out into the pressurised cabin; and dozens of gallons had accumulated at the bottom of the capsule".

"No, we didn't fall into the sea. Much to our disappointment, we decided to interrupt the flight because our closed space was saturated with toxic and flammable fumes".

"Yes, the meteorological conditions were very good and our flight path was ideal. At an altitude of 30,000 ft we were moving at 60 mph towards Algeria, where a strong and regular jet stream was going to push us around the world in sixteen days".

"Yes, we are sad and disappointed, but we mustn't forget that compared to other misfortunes in the world, this is a minor set-back".

"Yes, there is a recipe for not failing ever and that is…. not trying anything! And do you know the definition of success? Success is when you make at least one more attempt than the number of failures you've had!"

Was there going to be a *Breitling Orbiter 2*? All eyes turned to the sponsor. I already knew the answer thanks to a telephone call from Thedy Schneider, the owner of Breitling, who'd had these comforting words a few hours after the sea landing:

"The world didn't make itself in a day; there's no reason why we should manage to go round it at the first attempt!"

The marketing manager took over:

"Breitling has been taking part in the history of aviation for a century, making instruments for air professionals and chronographs for pilots. We know that history is built in successive stages and we will therefore stick to this project of a round-the-world balloon flight".

Over the next few days, we received nearly 18,000 messages of encouragement by post, telephone and e-mail. I could never have imagined such a wave of sympathy. It was obvious that, given the economic and social climate in which we lived, the public was touched by Breitling's perseverance and by the determination of our team which didn't give up despite the adversity.

At this stage, there were ten months left to launch the project again and rebuild the balloon completely. It would be ready for the winter 1997-98. The capsule, flooded with sea water during being towed to the coast, was beyond repair. I also had to make sure that all the partners I had gathered wanted to continue with the adventure.

So far, I hadn't had to convince anybody. All the members of the team had understood that this project was theirs as much as mine, they wanted to achieve what no one else had done before. That's the whole difference between persuasion and motivation. Throughout our life, decision-making involves a part of us which would rather refuse and another part which would rather accept. To persuade people, you have to fight against that part of them which wants to resist, to say no. To motivate them, you have to support that part which wants to say yes. If I had used up great arguments to show them why they had to follow me in this adventure, the recent failure would probably have put them off. On the contrary, by sharing the leadership of the project with the other members of the team, by wanting every one to work together rather than to work for my own dream, I had made them want to try something extraordinary.

Breitling had already replied, so had Don Cameron who was going to supply the equipment, and Alan Noble who directed the project. Without them, we couldn't go on.

Andy Elson, the chief technician in charge of the capsule which had gone so wrong, agreed to get back to work, but without hiding his personal ambition. He also dreamed of doing a trip round the world, and he had already planned his own flight with a Scottish millionaire. He even liked to say jokingly that Wim and I were the guinea pigs who tested the quality of his technique!

Météo Suisse and the Royal Institute of Meteorology were also going ahead. Pierre Eckert, who had done hundreds of path simulations for us, and Luc Trullemans, our guardian angel during the Chrysler Challenge, had enjoyed collaborating and comparing simulation results. They had defined the criteria for the expedition: departure would be in winter and in the northern hemisphere to make the most of regular jet streams; altitude: 30,000 to 33,000 ft; latitude: 30° to 40°.

Château-d'Œx village was going to do its best again to welcome the new balloon, just like Geneva International Airport, which would leave the same ground installations at our disposal for the monitoring of the next flight.

All was getting back into shape, but I still had to secure the collaboration of the International Olympic Committee. It was a major component, almost the frame of the puzzle. I had asked its President, Mr Juan Antonio Samaranch, to be the patron of my project in order to underline the symbolic dimension of that expedition. During a two-week flight, the time of an Olympic truce, *Breitling Orbiter* could become a nexus between all the countries in the world; I wanted to make the most of it to send a message of peace to their governments from the fax in the capsule. Therefore, I had knocked on that particular door to explain my humanitarian goal to its President, who had received me with arms wide open. But what would he say now that I had soaked the Olympic rings in the Mediterranean?

"Make the rings even more visible: your enterprise is a credit to the spirit of the Olympic movement", answered Mr Samaranch.

The feeling of responsibility towards our partners, our friends and even the public, intensified so much as the months went by that it became unbearable. Everybody had faith in us and was convinced that we would fully succeed. This was no longer my project, as when I'd first contacted Breitling; this wasn't even my team's project; it had become a universal project which now belonged to the public, because our dream was reflected in those of the public at large. A balloon lifting off to try and go round the planet, without an engine or a rudder, relying only on the extreme sophistication of advanced technology to play with the wind, became a paradoxical symbol in our materialistic society: it revived the myth of the impossible alliance between man and nature. Moreover, as the flight was to be non-stop, the scientific challenge added to the ecological one. The balloon had to remain in the air for two weeks to get a chance of doing a complete journey and every technical trick was needed. The challenge must have seduced the sponsor, who specialised in the manufacture of high technology timing instruments, as much as the rest of the team in charge of designing new inventions.

Apart from these fields, there was the historical side, of course. A flight like this had never been carried out before. At a time when continents, mountains and oceans had been discovered and explored, when aeroplanes criss-crossed the sky and satellites travelled into space, the press had every right in talking of the round-the-world balloon flight as if it were the last big adventure our world was going to live. Therefore, it was obvious that to Steve Fossett, Richard Branson and myself, the thought of writing a new page in history was more attractive than just reading what others had managed so far. An international competition, heavily stimulated by the media, had been launched and Steve was the big winner of the first round. Lifting off on his own from the United States two days after our failure and one week after Branson's, he had flown over the Atlantic, Africa, Arabia and India in an open cabin, snatching the record of duration from the Abruzzo family, with a flight that had lasted more than six days and covered over 9,000 miles! That was enough to shake the confidence of those who favoured a pressurised cabin!

That year, the list of American competitors grew fatter with the departure of Kevin Uliassi, on his own, and the duo Dick Rutan/ Richard Abruzzo. I was going to be reunited with my friend Richard in the air, but I didn't like the way in which the press was giving priority to the competition rather than to the symbolic nature of the flight. To cap it all, an American brewer had just announced a one-million dollar prize for the winner of the 'race of the century'. Whatever my wish had been, we had lost control of the events and were doomed to become the heroes or the victims of an enormous media machine. However, this wasn't going to change the atmosphere within our team or between the competitors. So far, I only knew Steve Fossett by telephone, and our relationship was based on mutual respect. Richard Branson had been a flying mate for years, we'd met at the Château-d'Œx International Hot-Air Balloon Festival.

Beyond the competition, and even beyond the symbol that was so dear to me, I had also found a piece of Ariadne's thread in that enterprise. I was reunited with the atmosphere known to me as a child, made of science and achievements, dreams and adventure. When I saw *Breitling Orbiter* emerge from the liquid helium vapour under the spotlights of a magical night, I was suddenly propelled back to the Cape Kennedy days. But this time, Wim and I were taking place in the capsule ready for the lift-off. It seemed quite normal to perpetrate an episode I was familiar with, at the risk of discovering its more painful aspects. I had been told of my grandfather's disappointment when he'd had to give up on his first departure to the stratosphere and deflate his balloon, exposed to the gibes of sceptical minds; or, when he'd been forced to interrupt the tests on his first bathyscaphe, which had crashed against the hull of the tug-boat.

Estelle, my eldest daughter, who had been very proud of having a 'famous dad', had also discovered the other side of the coin the day after the sea landing: she didn't want to go back to school because her friends had had the cheek to laugh at her father's misadventures. She'd been surprised to hear me say that I also found it ridiculous to 'fall' into the Mediterranean when you intend to do a tour around the world. She went back to school feeling reassured.

Anyway, the next time round we couldn't afford a new failure. Some technical modifications would have to be made, especially in the kerosene circuit which heated the helium at night. We still thought then that it was better to embark with liquid fuel rather than gas. Unlike propane, which had to be kept in heavy and bulky metal containers, kerosene could be stocked in big plastic bags which weighed very little.

The 175-ft tall envelope would follow the principle of the Rozière balloon whose lift depended on the rays of the sun during the day and the heat from the burners during the night. Combining helium with hot air had proved successful during the Chrysler Challenge and with Steve Fossett's extraordinary flight.

To increase the range of a balloon like that, you must try to minimise thermal differences, day and night. If the helium gets too hot under the effect of the sun, it starts overflowing, and if it loses too much heat through radiation during the night, the amount of fuel needed is very high. We were therefore going to cover the whole of the gas cell with an insulating material made of aluminised mylar, and protect the top of the balloon with a tent held into place by a secondary, smaller balloon, as we had done with *Orbiter 1*. To improve the efficiency even further, some ventilators plugged onto solar panels where going to propel cold air above and below the helium. Some seamstresses would have to sit behind their sewing machines, snowed under masses of white and silver fabric, to assemble the pieces of this colossal envelope.

Unfortunately, Wim was more concerned about the success of his hot-air balloon company in Belgium than about the preparations for the flight. He didn't make enough time to understand the improvements in the new capsule or to practise with the flight systems, which left him with some serious gaps. To overcome this lack of technical knowledge, and to ensure that I would have a reliable co-pilot to take over the controls while I slept, the team asked Andy to replace Wim on board. Mixing friendship with competence was a mistake but I didn't want to abandon my Atlantic team mate. How could I do that after all we'd gone through? In the end, Andy was going to join us, but this wasn't a satisfactory solution for anybody. Wim was disappointed not to be given the role he'd wanted, while Andy and I felt as if we had a passenger on board. Nevertheless, this was the only compromise which seemed acceptable at the time.

Adapting the capsule to the presence of a third man was no problem. There were already two berths, the second one would be used for sleep ing rather than storing equipment. But we had to add an oxygen bottle and another ten lithium filters to absorb carbon dioxide. Our pressurisation system was the same as the one my grandfather had invented for his stratospheric ascents. Closing the main porthole at a chosen altitude, usually around 8,000 to 10,000 ft, made it possible to keep a constant pressure, provided the capsule was hermetically sealed. The diffusion of oxygen in the closed atmosphere compensated the oxygen consumed by the crew, and lithium hydroxide cartridges absorbed the carbon dioxide produced by breathing. If a problem arose, a liquid nitrogen supply ensured that the cabin could be pressurised again several times without having to descend below 10,000 ft. The shape of the cabin was also familiar to me: a cylinder with two hemispheres, about 17 ft long with a 7.5 ft diameter, directly inspired by my father's pocket submarine, the *F.-A. Forel*.

Brian Jones, one of Andy's friends engaged by Cameron to supervise the building of the capsule, had organised the survival training of the crew at an English air base. It involved immersions in a cage similar to a cockpit, drops with a parachute over a swimming pool, handling life-jackets and life-boats, experiencing hypoxia in a depressurised atmosphere etc.

At the beginning of the jet stream season, all the equipment was transported to Château-d'Œx for the last elements to be assembled. In a corner of the workshop, cartons of freeze-dried food, a hundred and twenty bottles of water and bags of personal belongings all waited to be loaded. Steve Fossett was seething with impatience in Saint-Louis and tension could be felt in the streets of Château-d'Œx, which bore the effigies of *Breitling Orbiter 2*.

Richard Branson must have been monitoring the situation. Keen on being the first at trying his luck, he had seized the chance of a minute weather window to try and inflate his balloon in Marrakech. The winter before that, I'd already had to witness his lift-off, sitting helplessly before my television set. The race was launched, even if we kept on telling the journalists who invaded our workshop that this wasn't going to change anything for us:

"We are not struggling against the others but against technical problems".

"It's definitely easier to finish assembling the capsule on the ground than in the air, and we won't leave until everything is ready", added Andy with his English sense of humour.

My phone rang, it was a director from Breitling in England, who was terribly sorry to have to inform me that the Virgin balloon had just lifted off. I tried to reassure her:

"It doesn't matter, Victoria, we'll be going soon…"

"The balloon went… without the crew! The envelope lifted off alone. I called you at once. Richard doesn't even know yet!"

We couldn't believe he'd had such a stroke of bad luck. Some brutal turbulence had wrenched the ropes off the envelope while it was being inflated, and it was now flying 40,000 ft above the Atlas.

For weeks, Richard Branson and his team had assured us they didn't want to lift off before getting the authorisation to fly over China. They had even asked us to dissuade Fossett from leaving before the Chinese had given a positive answer. And suddenly, Richard was inflating his gigantic balloon in full daytime in the desert. The microclimate of the desert is often treacherous, including for those who try and startle their competitors. Let's face it, in a way, it was a case of the tables being turned!

What upset us, though, were the successive bad weather fronts which crossed the Alps during the month of December. We knew the 'El Niño' phenomenon was likely to disturb the climate, but not to that extent. We could stay and polish up the preparations, but we really wanted to lift off.

On 31st December, we were still on the ground at midnight, but neither Steve Fossett nor Kevin Uliassi were celebrating New Year's Eve with their family. They had both lifted off at dusk and were heading towards the Atlantic. The next morning, we learned with stupor that Kevin's helium cell, built by Cameron like ours, had burst and that Kevin had been forced to do an emergency

147

landing. As for *Solo Spirit*, it was going to beat all the speed records. Flying over an impressive storm, taking the thoughtless risk of emptying his tanks full of propane above the ground in order to fly higher, Steve had crossed the Atlantic in 44 hours but was heading towards Russia, which had forbidden his flight over its territory. His heating then broke down, followed apparently by the automatic pilot. Badly affected by the time spent at an altitude of 26,000 ft without pressurisation, Steve had to interrupt his flight and land on the shores of the Black Sea.

When I saw on television the pictures of the storm which was devastating Europe over which *Solo Spirit* had flown, I got very worried about Steve. But he was all right in the end, although he hadn't beaten either of the two records he'd set the year before.

Still stuck on the ground because of the bad weather, we were beginning to regret our decision to leave from Switzerland; but just then, Pierre and Luc gave the alarm. All of a sudden, it was the same feverish atmosphere as for the previous lift-off. Part of the team was busying itself around the capsule filling the fuel and gas tanks, while the rest was already preparing the envelope on the lift-off site. Meanwhile, the press relations department received the representatives of 230 media, among a forest of satellite dishes which grew like mushrooms. Château-d'Œx had become the centre of the world, but what mattered most to me was to resist the enormous pressure from journalists who already treated us like heroes.

"The world has its eyes set on your flight; how do you feel?"

"Has any museum expressed the wish to have your capsule on show yet?"

"Do you realise that if you succeed you'll be mentioned in encyclopaedias, next to Lindbergh and Armstrong?"

This was the type of question we'd grown to hate; they cruelly reminded us of our strong desire to succeed while there was nothing else we could do but go on with the preparations. All I wanted was to concentrate on the lift-off procedure and empty my mind to forget what was at stake in that enterprise.

The weather was splendid, but as the crucial time approached, the winds didn't take a southern direction as planned. A jet stream was passing vertically overhead the Alps and would have taken us to Japan in four days, but that would have involved going across China, and they still hadn't given their authorisation, despite a year and a half of political and administrative approaches. We couldn't grab this extraordinary stroke of luck and had to postpone the lift-off.

The next day, the simulations came up with some paths which avoided China; we decided to launch the operation. This is when the most incredible thing occurred in front of a terrified crowd: during the unloading on the lift-off site, the cables holding the capsule gave way... it crashed on the trailer with a sinister thundering noise, followed by a dead silence. Thinking he'd done something wrong, the driver panicked, jumped out of the crane, ran away and disappeared in the snow. In fact, it was one of Cameron's subcontractors who'd done something wrong; the crimping on four of his eight cables had slipped out. Solicitors were going to have a field day!

I never thought I could ever have felt more ashamed and ridiculous than when I'd ended up floating in the Mediterranean with *Orbiter 1*. Now I saw it was possible... this mission was truly teaching me to lose all touchiness and sensitivity with regards to criticism.

Sitting before the world press, which hesitated between labelling us as 'amateurish' or 'cursed', we tried to dissipate a misunderstanding:

"It is quite obvious that what happened is totally inadmissible. Besides, you must realise that a round-the-world balloon flight requires more than known and tested technology. We will fly with materials specially created for this mission and which have nothing to do with usual aerostats".

In fact, we weren't going to fly at all, we had to repair the cabin and test all the equipment. The crisis of confidence couldn't be ignored: the cables could have given way during the flight...

Richard Branson rang me immediately:

"Richard, we lost our capsule after you lost your envelope. I think you're the only one who can understand how I feel..."

"Yes, Bertrand, but when you wake up tomorrow and realise you're still alive, I promise you you'll be very happy!"

The next day, Andy, Wim and I were still alive, our cabin had been taken to the workshop and Dick Rutan was lifting off in Albuquerque with Dave Melton, who had replaced Abruzzo. We thought we'd really missed our chance, until an unbelievable development took place. After an hour's flight, the *Global Hilton* helium cell burst like Uliassi's and the two pilots preferred to abandon their balloon in the air and use their parachute. Images of their enormous balloon crashing then exploding against electric power lines were extensively broadcast on the news.

What curse had been invoked on this journey round the world? What was our next attempt going to be like? The jet stream season was coming to an end and we would have to seize the next weather window as soon as our capsule was repaired. Aware of our preoccupation, the Breitling head office sent me the following message:

"We don't want to put any pressure on you to lift off this winter. You, and you alone, have to decide on that, and you must do so on flight criteria not on marketing requirements".

Then all went very quickly. After a few false hopes which reminded me of the long wait before the Chrysler Challenge, meteorologists put us on standby for 28th January 1998, which coincided with my grandfather's birthday. Surely, destiny couldn't play a nasty trick on me that day!

It was the third rehearsal and everybody knew exactly what had to be done. This allowed me to stand back a bit, despite the feeling that this time the stakes were even greater. I was drawn between the desire to enjoy every second of this extraordinary day and the need to withdraw into myself to avoid rejoicing too much. In any case, I was sick and tired of saying for the umpteenth time over a microphone what my motivations were and, especially, why I thought we were going to succeed. I didn't feel like being a hero at all.

On the last night, Andy and the technicians kept busy, Alan Noble had sent me to sleep for a few hours. I didn't see *Orbiter 2* take shape among curls of icy condensation. Nor did I see the wind cast the 175 ft long envelope to the ground in front of firemen and voluntary workers from the Château-d'Œx Balloon Club. The Carbagaz specialists had to work between gusts to blow in the liquid helium after evaporating it in large radiators. Their boss, Roland Wicky, remained in close contact with Cameron's employees:

"There is only one problem: I understand their English but they don't understand mine!"

During the night, spectators, technicians and journalists had pulled together to face the −4°F. Each of them felt personally involved in the project; so much so that a television commentator reported live:

"Here, in Château-d'Œx, 'we' have now finished inflating the balloon".

It was Kevin Uliassi who woke me up to tell me over the phone that he was worried about the envelope:

"I just wanted to tell you that Cameron didn't understand why my balloon burst. You ought to have your helium cell modified".

"Too late, Kevin, my balloon is already inflated and I'm lifting off in two hours".

"Sorry, I didn't know…"

A shiatsu session the night before had relieved the flu-symptoms which had been bothering me for two days, but my stomach had been in a knot since my arrival on the site. My mouth felt so dry I could barely swallow the piece of croissant I was trying to eat. I cannot describe the unbelievable emotion I felt when I saw, from miles away, the silvery silhouette of *Orbiter 2* against the dark mass of the Alps. The instant was unreal, magical, timeless; an absolute dream which nonetheless made me shiver with fear and respect. I was very moved to find my family and all my friends reunited around the frosted orange capsule. I was split between my desire to spend that last moment with them, the wish to empty my mind and concentrate, and the need to answer every question, producing clouds of condensation with every word:

"This time, I won't believe in the lift-off until the ropes have been cut!"

"If there is a stowaway on board, it will be a technical incident…"

"Yes, I am scared. I had the choice between feeling scared considering the whole enterprise or being mad enough not to perceive the immense difficulty of the task. I chose to be scared!"

I spent a long time with the French navigator Olivier de Kersauson. He knew what a departure for a trip around the world was like. He confessed that he preferred to disconnect the day before the boarding, to reduce the tension. Then he added these touching words:

"You're our ambassador. There is no need for you to have stage fright because, in a way, we're all going aboard with you!"

The sight of my three little girls in front of the balloon was heart rending. They looked so innocent! For Michèle and my father, or for my brother and my sister, things were different; adults have a more rational vision of what goes on. A year before, Oriane, aged four, had confessed:

"When dad went away in a balloon, I felt sad…"

I wanted to lift off because I knew that I would only feel better once I was in the air, but a satellite aerial needed to be repaired. Time was going even more slowly for the poor radio and TV announcers who had been reporting live for two hours already, during which all was at a standstill. Andy was overworked, Wim was giving a last interview and shed a few tears. Some sailing friends looked at me with a twinkling in their eyes, here they were, totally fascinated by that balloon which seemed to already inspire them for their next feats.

Pierre and Luc gave me the latest weather forecast. It was the same as the day before: we had to do a very slow flight towards Egypt, to climb into the jet streams three days later.

The solar panels were now connected, the aerial was repaired, and the Château-d'Œx hot-air balloon had just lifted off to probe the local thermal inversion layers. It was time to give the farewell speech before climbing into the capsule:

"Last year, to encourage us to continue with our project, some school children sent us this quote from Belgian poet Maurice Carème: 'The earth is round so that peace, friendship and love can go round it some day'. This morning, Andy, Wim and I will bear it in mind as we lift off. If our flight is a success, it will be your success too. If we fail, we will be particularly sad to have failed you. But the most precious reward for this trip round the world is here already: it is your friendship, the quality of the messages we've received from all five continents, to accompany us to the sky. Thank you for joining in our dream".

I then tried to kiss my family goodbye without making it too obvious that my head was already somewhere else. It was both fascinating to be going at last and heartbreaking to leave them with tears frosting on their cheeks. Yet, dozens of cameras made it impossible to have any intimacy.

Michèle had understood it, looking very serious between two forced smiles, when a journalist reminded her quite rightly that a balloon had been shot down by a military helicopter in Belarus:

"What worries me most is the political question. But now I want to see them go. He'll feel all right up there. This is the end of years of preparation and the beginning of a dream".

The sky was now perfectly clear and the silver glints of our balloon had turned to a deeper grey in the shadow which the mountains projected over the valley. I grabbed the ladder with both hands and climbed every step with a mixed feeling of determination and fatalism. After one last waving of the hand, standing on the capsule and secretly praying for all to end well, I finally settled inside. I went over the check-list, my heart pounding. Wim joined me in the cockpit, Andy put his harness on near the burners. From the shouts of the public, I knew they were climbing the ladder. Everything went in slow motion, but in a very orderly manner. Carbagaz disconnected the last helium tube and Don detached the second overflow tube. Olivier de Kersauson lit the burners with the Olympic torch. I had strongly insisted on this mythical flame symbolically going around the world.

Time suddenly froze. I had to give the go ahead for the departure. Wim and Andy were ready; with a broken voice, I told Don and Alan that they could free the balloon. An incredible clamour rose from the launch site and made me realise that we were lifting off. A clamour I would never forget; it seemed to be lifting our monster up in the air. The loud applause covered the sound of the village bells before the noise of helicopter rotors took over. Andy spread out the aerials and positioned the solar panels while I began firing the burners to penetrate the thermal inversion layer which slowed down our ascent. The amount of work to be done on board and the concentration that was needed to leave the valley prevented us from thoroughly enjoying the emotional discharge we had been waiting for months; however, a few knowing glances between us were enough to share this happy instant.

Down below, emotion had reached its peak. Later, I was told that even some journalists seemed deeply moved. Satellite dishes sent enthusiastic comments from one end of the world to the other, as if to get there before us:

"Here, in Château-d'Œx, a page of the history of aviation is being written!"

"*Breitling Orbiter 2* has set off on a sublime revolution; wouldn't we all love to secretly visit the land of jet streams with them?"

I continued using the burners until the sun took over. Andy had joined me and we closed the porthole when reaching 8,000 ft. It was now time to inform the air-traffic controllers:

"Geneva Delta from Balloon Hotel Bravo – Quebec Bravo Victor. Have lifted off from Château-d'Œx, climbing 400 feet per minute to flight level 250, heading: 230°, speed: 10 knots".

"Hello Breitling Orbiter, Geneva Delta speaking. Receiving you loud and clear. Have a good flight".

The Swiss Control officer sounded somewhat relieved. Last year, the kerosene leak had provoked a short-circuit affecting several instruments, and we had crossed the Geneva airport approach zone blindly.

We reached 25,000 ft rather delicately, slowing down the ascent several times with the valve. It was at this stage, when reaching the ceiling, that Rutan's and Uliassi's envelopes had burst. I felt fully confident and didn't once look at my parachute folded on a berth.

However, a strange whistling noise worried us. Going round the cabin, we realised that there was a leak in the back porthole.

It had been badly fitted during the icy night when the balloon had been inflated. The system was conceived to open towards the outside and provide an emergency exit with a parachute, it was impossible to fit it again from the inside. I was furious, but had to contain myself to avoid poisoning the atmosphere on board... we looked at each other, embarrassed. We could hear the air leak, and the pressure of the cabin dropped dangerously. We had to put our oxygen masks on and inform the flight control centre of the problem. Alan, Brian and Mel had just got there in a helicopter to join Sue and still had their anoraks on. In any case, there was nothing they could do for us.

I had the strange feeling of being cut off from the world, as if in one of those hypnotic experiences which create a spatiotemporal distortion. It felt as if we'd left ages ago, as if we'd always lived in that capsule, when in fact we'd only left two hours before. The wind was slow, very slow. We were moving at 11 mph, and we could still see Château d'Œx. The enormous envelope could be spotted hundreds of miles around, but we were almost motionless!

Andy and I tried to repair the leak with mastic and plastic bags, but that didn't work. We descended again to 20,000 ft then 16,000 ft to be able to remove our oxygen masks, and reached Megève after a 10 hour-flight. The sun had set over the Alps, which were now turning red. Many airliners made a detour to come and admire our shiny ball which competed with the evening star: some brief radio contacts were made with the captains who surprised their passengers with an unusual show before we disappeared into the dark night.

We started taking turns to use the two berths. Andy was seized by a headache which lasted for three days during which he had to lie down most of the time! After sleeping for four hours, I was back in the cockpit on my own, in front of a GPS which indicated a speed of 9 mph. What a depressing first night. We weren't progressing, the kerosene consumption seemed enormous and the sudden isolation cruelly contrasted with all the agitation of the lift-off. We were abandoned to ourselves and to the wind. Wrapped up in my anorak, I was feeling a bit down and secretly hoped that future nights wouldn't be so long.

When daylight returned, I wondered what landscape it would reveal. We were leaving the Alpes-Maritimes region and going along the French Riviera. We would be flying over it all morning at an altitude of 10,000 ft: how strange to be dragged at 10 knots on a panoramic excursion over the beaches. The wind was just as slow; it changed direction and pushed us towards Corsica. I now recalled the first day of the Chrysler Challenge, full of upsets and unforeseen events. I knew we had to take things as they came.

Our means of communication worked well, the satellite telephone allowed us to give our first live interviews, and we even managed to transmit some filmed images to a plane which had come from Saint-Tropez to meet us. Unfortunately, the kerosene circuit on the starboard side wasn't working so well, there was a dramatic drop in the pressure. An inspection carried out by Andy along the outer ladder didn't reveal any leak, we had no explanation for it.

We were permanently in touch with the air-traffic controllers as we were cutting through several approach zones, and, when we got near Corsica the radio crackled one more time:

"Breitling balloon from Yellow Rascals".

"Yellow Rascals, hello, HB-QBV speaking".

"We are coming to say hello, will be in sight in two minutes".

And 120 seconds later, we heard the roaring noise of their reactors. Two Crusaders from the French air force formed a patrol in the misty evening. They were so close I could see the heads of the pilots turning round to look at us, from under their canopies.

"Breitling, your balloon is superb!"

"Thanks for your visit, Yellow Rascals".

We were reaching Corsica, the sun was setting over the sea and I was sitting outside the capsule, with a camera in my hand. The panorama included the Alps, the Pyrenees and the snowy summits of the beautiful island. I was happy to share it all with Wim, who had come to join me. We weren't doing a round-the-world flight so far, but it was a magnificent flight in a balloon. The wind was so weak, I didn't know where we would get to, but I had an inkling that we would fly for a long time.

Andy spent most of the night at the controls and felt that time was dragging even more. He tried hard to solve the problem with the fuel circuit, and admitted that he would be more efficient once his headache had cleared. Being a big coffee and Coca-Cola drinker, he must have suffered from the rationing of caffeine!

Dawn was like an extraordinary symphony of colours caressing hundreds of small islands in the Bonifacio estuary. I spent the day looking for the best currents and checking the weather forecast. The best layer was 500 ft thick, just less than three times the height of the balloon! Maintaining our altitude sharply was a subtle and delicate affair; we had to anticipate the very slow reactions of our immense mass of helium. As soon as I drifted away from the correct level, I entered a different airstream with a new speed and direction, followed by a lateral wind which made the envelope flap like a sail.

The solar panels provided a lot of energy which we used for telephone interviews, the transmission of photos taken on board and for warm water. This way, we could stick some bags of vacuum-packed pre-cooked food into the kettle.

The main meal was fillet of ostrich garnished with rice and vegetables. This 'red' meat, from organic farming in Australia, had just landed on the European market. It was bound to become very popular as it contained very little fat and was much healthier than our western meat full of hormones. Being practically a vegetarian, Andy had already started using the bags of freeze-dried food.

Our early evening meal could have varied from the intended menu that day; air-traffic controllers in Naples had just invited us to have some spaghetti with them! They seemed very disappointed when we explained that we couldn't land at the foot of their control tower and go back the next day with our stomachs full.

The fax Brian sent us from Geneva was less politically correct but just as funny:

"You are now overhead Naples. Make the most of it to throw all your rubbish overboard; nobody in town will notice the difference!"

Our reply was invariably the same:

"We'd rather you told us where the wind is, we're still looking for it!"

During the night, the airstreams finally became worthy of that name, going at a speed of 30 mph towards the south-east. For the first time, the faxes we received from the weather experts mentioned the names of distant countries such as Iran, Pakistan, India, which we could reach if we flew at an altitude of 30,000 ft. We would have to fix the porthole.

Andy felt better and wanted to stretch his legs. With his climbing gear, plus a parachute, he embarked on an extra-vehicular excursion which was the object of much media coverage. The possibility of ascending towards the jet streams announced for the next day or so depended on his success. The scene was impressive. 5000 ft above the Adriatic, he let himself slide under the capsule, and secured the frame of the porthole to a strap. If he dropped it, it would be the end of the flight. Fortunately, we were flying through some clouds which reduced the feeling of vertigo. Lying on my stomach in the cabin, I could now open the dome and check the rubber seal. Out in the icy air, Andy had to make a tremendous effort not to slip on the curvature of the hull. He replaced the dome in its groove. I was then able to lock it from the inside, after tightening the clamp just to make sure. Andy gathered all his strength to climb back up with a system of pulleys and joined us to try and warm up. Photographs taken during the operation were immediately sent by satellite to the flight control centre, but Andy, who's an honest guy, told me in a low voice:

"Instead of all that publicity, I'd rather have closed that blasted porthole correctly in the first place!"

A progressive ascent up to 30,000 ft confirmed the quality of the repair. The temperature outside was nearing - 49°F while in the cabin it was + 68°F. We could at last enjoy the safety and comfort of pressurisation, especially as the meteorological conditions were evolving positively. Our speed increased to 78 mph, we overflew Albania, Greece, Turkey, Syria and Iraq, and arrived over Iran after 36 hours.

We often had to change altitude to adapt to the best airstreams, this is why we happened to be very close to Mount Olympus just as the sun was setting.. The flame of the burners, lit three days ago with the Olympic Torch, was now level with the cloudy summit. What a marvellous way for it to return to its origins!

A good deal of our time was taken up establishing contacts with air-traffic controllers, whose accents varied as the hours went by. They didn't fully understand the nature of that big mass moving so slowly across their radar screens. Because of a small mistake in the flight path calculations, we were pushed towards Syria and Iraq, which were not in our flight plan. Getting an authorisation from Syria had been no problem thanks to the efficiency of Swiss Control in Geneva, but we could sense that our ground team was worried at the thought of us overflying Iraq, right across an exclusion zone. Military tension with the United States was at its height

"I accept to find no answers, I accept to be nourished by doubt and let the unknown take hold of my inner world".

"May the spiritual world and the human world harvest the fruit of great achievements" (Burmese maxim).

"For twenty days always advancing in the same direction to finally come back to the starting point… and be forever changed". (Take-off of Breitling Orbiter 3.)

"On the other side of the frosted porthole, there is the light of the rising sun. On the other side of the visceral fear of the unknown, there is the spirit of adventure".

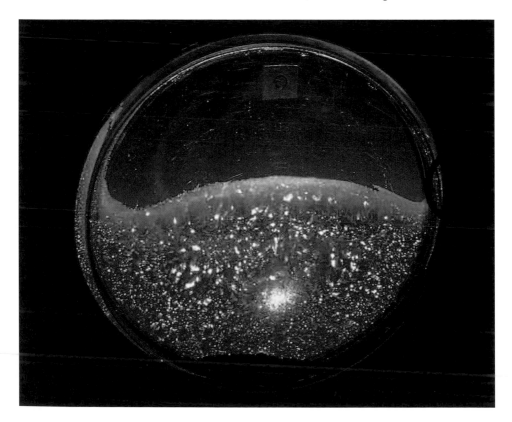

Winds of Hope
Foundation
(www.windsofhope.org)

"It was the wind, the wind of Providence, which carried us both, Brian and me. From now on, and forever, this wind will be the wind of Hope for us. And we shall do all that we can to make it blow stronger around the earth".

"By writing a sequel to the history of aviation, without fuel or pollution, Solar Impulse intends to be a contribution to the promotion of renewable energies by the world of exploration and adventure".

and Alan gave us a piece of advice over the phone, with his usual black humour:

"Try and get to Baghdad before the Americans, it will be a lot quieter! And make a note of the US Air Force radio frequency: they're the ones you'll have to convince not to shoot you down; the Iraqis have no anti-aircraft defence left!"

The Syrian air-traffic controller confirmed he had no contacts with his Iraqi counterpart and told us politely not to count on him to announce our arrival.

I timidly pressed the broadcasting button:

"Baghdad Control from Olympic Balloon HB-QBV, do you copy?"

"Olympic Balloon from Baghdad Control, go ahead".

"Hello, Baghdad. We are going to cross your territory at an altitude of 30,000 ft, heading: 100 degrees, speed: 70 knots".

I waited for the reply with awe, counting every second that went by, but my interlocutor didn't sound worried at all:

"OK, Olympic Balloon. Call Baghdad again when you leave the Iraqi territory. Have a good flight".

I felt like crying with joy, but as Andy and Wim were asleep, I could only share my relief with the journalists who were all asking for a live interview. For CNN, that was the scoop of the day. A balloon pushed by the wind over what was the most militarised region at the time was involuntarily drawing the world's atten tion to the value of peace, a few hours before a possible American intervention.

A thick layer of clouds covered the whole country. I tried to imagine what war would be like. A few pilots, sitting comfortably in a cockpit similar to ours, would send a shower of missiles at the touch of a button. Our air-traffic controller would probably be among their first victims, and his family, assuming he still had one, would never see him again. The dead bodies of men, women and children would be scattered in the streets full of smoke and rubble. The wounded, feeling terrorised, would be screaming with pain like you never hear them in Hollywood films. As for the dictators, they would be safe in a bunker as always. But, worst of all, after a few days of initial curiosity, life in the world would resume its course and people would start getting worried about another crisis. Once the war was over, nobody would remember the suffering of those shattered families or think of the wounded and terribly mutilated people. Yet, they would have to endure years of sadness and difficulty. War was despicable. Even more so when it seems to be forgotten as soon as you change channel or turn off the television. Even if I knew nothing of this air-traffic controller apart from his anonymous voice, I silently wished him good luck and sent a prayer to the sky for him. I was so close that it may even have heard me. I sincerely hoped that the great and the good in the world would come to an agreement to spare the ordinary people from, yet again, being the victims of human barbarism.

I thought it was time to broadcast our message of peace to all countries, through the national Olympic committees. Our flight would then help to do more than just setting new records.

Urgent and personal message to all Presidents of the national Olympic committees (or their representative)

Dear Sir,

Following the letter sent on 4th December 1997 by Juan-Antonio Samaranch, President of the International Olympic Committee, we are delighted and honoured to send you, from the satellite fax in our balloon, this message of peace which we would like you to pass on to the newspapers, radio stations and television channels of your country, with a brief explanatory note:

Our balloon has just lifted off from Switzerland, headquarters of the International Olympic Committee which is the patron of our attempt to make the first non-stop trip round the earth. In fact, we should rather say round our planet, because, seen from above, the set of shapes and colours which form the plains, the mountains, the rivers and the oceans call for respect.

We have no engine on board, the wind and the wind only is what pushes us towards your country. We may fly over it, or, the airstreams may lead us in another direction. At any rate, the wind allows our balloon to become a nexus between all countries in the world for a few days, as well as the ambassador of the Olympic ideal based on peace, mutual comprehension and solidarity. But above all, we are motivated by a desire to communicate with the inhabitants of every country in order to tell them what we can see from above.

When we watch the immense vault of heaven from which our balloon is hanging, we cannot but admire with modesty and humility this vast complex which mankind belongs to. Our planet is in a small corner of the universe and we may look lovingly at Nature, the cradle in which human beings come to the world, grow up and die. We cannot but feel how lucky human beings are to be able to live there, or rather, how lucky they would be if they started living in harmony with their environment, with their neighbours, with themselves.

Seen from the sky, no mountain looks like any other, no river forms the same path as any other, and we know full well that no human being is the same as any other. This is what makes our planet so marvellously rich and, at the same time, what causes the most awful conflicts. And yet, all human beings have their feet on earth and their head in the sky, just like a river takes its source in the mountains. It flows towards the sea and human beings follow their destiny. They try to follow their own path in their own way. They can choose the way of war and blood or they can choose the way of blossoming through tolerance, sport and the innocent smile of a child. Every man can choose his path, and gain the altitude he needs to acquire a better understanding of the meaning of life.

Today, our path crossed yours and tomorrow, the wind will push us towards another country. We shall continue with our flight and you will continue with your life which is also a great adventure. In the end, we are probably all seeking some guidance.

We have to say goodbye already, but please help us to spread this message of peace around our planet. It needs it badly.'

> *The pilots of the 'Breitling Orbiter 2' Olympic balloon*
> *Bertrand Piccard (Switzerland)*
> *Wim Verstraeten (Belgium)*
> *Andy Elson (United Kingdom)*

The Iraqi sky was immensely empty, the radio desperately silent, and the sea of clouds still stretching endlessly. I was the only one to speak with Baghdad Control in a heavy and barren atmosphere. We were about to leave the country and called Teheran. On the other side of the frontier, we had a major surprise. Nobody understood how we could be coming out of nowhere. When we informed them of our position and gave an Iraqi city as a point of reference, a deadly silence made us realise that the blackout between the two countries was so absolute that Iranian maps didn't include their neighbouring country! We weren't particularly worried because Iran had given us permission to overfly its territory, in a letter starting with 'In the name of the Almighty'. It was the first time we received a letter from so high above!

As to the rest of the flight, the atmosphere on board reflected our doubts. A fax informed us that we might reach the Californian coast in seven days, which would be fabulous. But that would mean crossing China. We knew that in the meantime, in Europe, the British, Belgian and Swiss governments were doing their best to get the go ahead which would save our flight. Without this authorisation, in theory, we could continue at a lower altitude towards Indochina and go round China from the south. However, the winds were so slow that this would entail a two-week detour, and then we couldn't be sure to catch up with the jet stream over the Pacific Ocean.

During the following night, Andy managed to find a remedy for the failure of the starboard kerosene circuit, which involved short-circuiting one of the two pressure accumulators. This meant that the pilot doing the night shift would have to open and close a valve situated under the floor board every three minutes and a half. That should make him stay awake!

Before going to sleep for a few hours, I called Michèle again. It was the 1st of February and the first time in twenty years that I spent that day without her…

The day after, we had to check the level of our propane supplies as we'd used it in conjunction with the kerosene far more often than planned. Since the inspection could only be carried out from the outside, we let the balloon descend and opened the top dome. We were flying over the immense salt desert which stretches across the Iranian territory. It only took one minute to connect the pipe from the first to the second tank, but we wanted to enjoy the fresh air over this breathtaking panorama for a while. As we were taking some photographs, we suddenly noticed some sheets of ice detaching themselves from the surface of the envelope. It must have been the first time in centuries that snow fell over that desert, but it also meant that our balloon had frosted up and was therefore heavier. That explained our excessive consumption of kerosene. After letting the ice melt under the Iranian sun and closing the porthole, we returned to a cruising altitude. Reappearing on the radar screens of the air-traffic controllers, we received the following message:

"To HB-QBV from Iran Air Force 79. We order you to land at the nearest airport for identification. Contact Birjand on 121.7 or Kirman on 112.5".

This was a big blow. I got hold of the microphone and risked my all.

"To Iran Air Force 79, from the Olympic balloon trying to do a non-stop round-the-world flight. We are being pushed by the wind and cannot land now. Swiss Control in Geneva will confirm our flight plan if you ask them".

When I informed Alan immediately after, he sounded worried. The news was broadcast as dozens of journalists were hanging around at the control centre. CNN decided to approach the Iranian authorities directly.

In the meantime, the Sabena flight from Bangkok to Brussels intervened on the same frequency but in French:

"To Breitling balloon from Sabena. This is the captain speaking. Don't be defeated. There is no way you should interrupt your superb flight. Good luck!"

The wide-ranging interventions were successful. After half an hour of uncertainty, we received this brief answer:

"To HB-QBV, from Iran Air 376: Teheran gives you authorisation to continue with your flight"

The looks we exchanged expressed our relief. We could now head for Afghanistan, with a superb sunset which lit a mass of animal-shaped clouds from behind.

The falling night gave us the impression of flying over a country which no longer existed. Kabul didn't reply to our calls, despite many attempts on various frequencies and the relay offered by several Swissair, Singapore Airline and Air India aeroplanes. What we did learn from the latter is that they were flying over Karachi in a jet stream blowing at a speed of 170 mph! We would be there the next day, but we could only take advantage of it if the Chinese gave us the go ahead. Meanwhile, we were flirting with a lateral branch of this current, at an altitude of 26,000 ft and moving at 72 mph. Some wind shear provoked by speed and direction gradients was shaking the balloon from all sides, and some violent turbulence swept the flames of the burners, putting them out on several occasions. While we were lighting them again, the balloon descended several thousand feet at a time. All of this was taking place over a high mountain range, surrounded with threatening clouds hardly lit up by a shy moon.

"Alan, this is Andy speaking, we are crossing a zone of violent turbulence".

"How serious, Andy?"

"Well, to give you an idea, Bertrand ordered us to get the parachutes ready!"

"..."

To ease the atmosphere a bit, Brian sent us this fax:

"You are now flying over a country where people have some strange customs. At weddings, men start dancing in a circle while screaming and shooting in the air with old guns. If you are invited to one of these ceremonies, we suggest you refuse and continue with your journey!"

We had a fantastic team. People were doing twelve-hour shifts, ready to do their best to solve every problem, but also to add their touch of humour in moments of tension or tediousness.

We had to choose another altitude to avoid the layer of turbulence which could make us crash against those mountain peaks below, but we felt trapped. If we went higher, the mass of air would be calmer but would take us to Tibet at galloping speed. From a political viewpoint this would be the worst course. If we went lower, our speed would decrease a lot but we would reach Pakistan and go round the Himalayas from the south.

Safety was the main thing. The next day, we reached the Indus plain and dragged ourselves over it at low altitude.

This message from Pierre and Luc sounded like Chinese torture:

'You have the choice between continuing at around 10,000 ft and fly over Benares in two days or, rising to the jet stream above you and reach Hawaii in four days and Mexico the day after. The Chinese specified that they would force you to land immediately if you entered their territory.'

For the second time round, we were under a favourable branch of the high altitude airstreams but, for political reasons, we couldn't make use of it. If only the jet streams were a bit more aware of our geostrategic problems!

We were to learn later that the Chinese prime minister was in Switzerland at the time, to promote his country at the World Economic Forum in Davos. The first topic of conversation with the federal councillors who received him had been the *Breitling Orbiter 2* flight. Negotiations were taking place at the highest level and the situation might improve for us. In the meantime, many Belgian schools were writing to the Chinese embassy in Brussels, and the British prime minister, Tony Blair, personally intervened on our behalf.

The agitation of our team at the other end of the world strangely contrasted with our state of mind in the capsule. We were as calm as the wind that pushed us. We faced the success or the failure of our whole enterprise with a certain detachment. In fact, it was impressive to see how we were able to stand back from all the bad news that came in. So far, we had embarked on an outstanding balloon expedition. Curiously, as our dream was doomed to failure I began to open up more to the philosophical experience of the flight.

Even if the Chinese changed their mind, we'd lost too much time flying at low altitude to finish off the journey. We could make it to America, but no further. I realised it without anger. Up in the air I was quite a different person… In fact, I felt no anger or suffering because I didn't cling to a goal which had become impossible to reach. That enabled me to open up to all that surrounded me and to everything I felt: the Indus valley stretching right across; the farms made of mud bricks and their occupants startled at seeing us appear in the morning mist; and above all, above all, the voice of the Pakistani air-traffic controller which resounded more in my heart than in my earphones:

"Olympic balloon from Karachi Control. You are approaching the Indian frontier. Contact Delhi on 124 decimal 55. Good luck, good flight and… God bless you".

God bless us… the emotion brought tears to my eyes. The technical jargon of radiotelephony had suddenly given way to another dimension. Indeed, I think God blessed us in enabling us to keep an open mind, to accept what life brought us rather than have the fierce determination to get what was good for our ego.

In silence, I also prayed for that Pakistani. Our worlds were so different, yet his three words did more good to me than I had been able to do in several weeks.

We were already a long way south and, although it was winter, the climate changed. Some enormous clouds were turning into cumulo-nimbus which every pilot dreads. Fortunately, the sunset cooled them down before they turned into a tropical storm.

Time had stopped completely, I lost all notion of it. I had to count on my fingers every time or turn the pages of the logbook to calculate our flying time.

But that day, the journalists reminded us about it. We had been in the air for over six days, 148 hours to be precise. This was the longest balloon flight in history. Steve Fossett phoned us to congratulate us on breaking his record. What a gentleman! His fax, received a bit later, touched us even more:

"You've had many problems during your flight and you solved them. In such circumstances, most pilots would have given up. Your determination and the quality of your resources show why a time record is important and why you fully deserve it. Steve".

Whatever happened now, our honour was safe. Still, we were miles away from wanting to break a record. I wanted to prolong the flight as much as possible to continue having that extraordinary sensation of inner peace, of serenity and detachment. I had spoken so much about it in my lectures and during my therapies that I was grateful to be so deeply immersed in it.

Andy, on the contrary, let us see that he was disheartened. He didn't think we would get anywhere and wanted... to land! For Wim and I, this was totally out of the question, but we didn't want to enter into a conflict. Making use of the metacommunication techniques we had developed before the departure, I told Andy how I felt:

'I've been working on this project for five years and I really want to be able to enjoy every minute of this flight. I hope you understand how important it is for me.'

'Bertrand, you know that when I am in a bad mood it doesn't last long. I'll probably be in a friendlier mood tomorrow.'

The next day, with a little help from destiny, the wind took us to one of the wonders of the world. I was lying on my berth when I heard Wim and Andy marvelling about 'an unbelievable thing' which made me open the curtains to pass my head through:

'Come and see that, we're above the Taj Mahâl!'

I jumped to the top of the cabin in my pyjamas, in the icy air of a winter morning, to see, 6,000 ft below, the white marble of this sublime tomb slipping silently into the soft rays of the rising sun.

We were fascinated and touched by this monument, as enormous as the love which Moghul emperor Shâh Jahân had felt for his wife, and watched it disappear into the mist.

A fax from Geneva cheered Andy up even more than that magical sight. Alan had perceived the danger of the situation and had written:

"Breaking the record of the longest flight in a balloon is one thing, but you still have to beat the absolute record of duration in any type of aircraft. Dick Rutan flew for nine days and four minutes in his *Voyager* when doing his trip round the world in an aeroplane. Let's see if you can do better!"

Cut to the quick, Andy rushed to his ruler and his protractor to calculate the extrapolations of our path. He added with a smile:

"You see, my bad moods never last for very long!"

To stay in the air a few more days, we would have to fly low, below 5,000 ft, otherwise, the winds would bring us back towards the Himalayas and China again. I no longer thought of the jet streams blowing at 150 mph above our heads, the magic of this privileged contact with India had totally absorbed me. Sitting outside, I was watching the houses and the rice fields, the rocky mountains and the meanders of the river Yamuna pass by in absolute silence, like a dream. Through the telephoto lens, villages looked like Vasarely's paintings with the colours missing. The artist had only used shades of beige and grey. As we were flying at the lower limit of a thermal inversion layer, the air rising from the ground couldn't go higher and the smells it carried had concentrated at our level. The mixture of fragrances so typical of India, a blend of spices, incense, filth and hot dust reached us. We were no longer flying above the country but 'in' it, among its people.

Towards the evening, an Indian Piper came to circle our reddening balloon. An English TV channel had bet we would land in Benares and had rented an aeroplane to film us live.

The following night was to be the most turbulent of all, the wind shear from Afghanistan was almost forgotten. We had expected to have a quiet time after such a peaceful day, but we blindly came across the remnants of active cloud rains. The flames of the burners were put out, the inertia of the balloon made us bounce like a yo-yo. We seemed to be using all the space in the sky to control our disorderly vertical movements which we couldn't control.

The next morning, we tried to fly lower and gain a few more degrees to the south. We were flying level at an altitude of 1,000 ft when, in a moment of distraction on my part, the balloon descended to 150 feet. Firing the burners to the maximum, I managed to redress the situation before we touched the ground. Andy, who had been watching the manoeuvre from outside to throw a bag of ballast, found himself face to face with a farmer busy digging his field. Dishevelled and unshaven but nonetheless polite, he greeted the Indian man with a timid 'hello' which provoked an unexpected reaction: as if some extraordinary demon from his mythology had suddenly appeared before him, the farmer quickly picked up his shovel and ran away across the fields.

The scene was amusing and I reported it with delight during the live interviews given by satellite every day. Technical progress is amazing. Five years ago, establishing contacts from the Atlantic through radio waves redirected to a telephone via a specialised coastal station was quite an achievement. Nowadays, I just had to dial a number and wait for my interlocutor to pick up his telephone. My father was taking part in several programmes, which made it easy for us to keep in touch. It must have felt strange for him to remain on the firm ground after organising so many expeditions. In fact, he once admitted that perhaps he wouldn't have gone so many times if he'd known how hard it was for those who waited for him. I realised more than ever how courageous Michèle was, bringing up the family as if nothing unusual was happening, to protect our children from the consequences of the media coverage. Discreet but not a bit passive, she knew every detail of the project which she had been sharing with me from the beginning. She went to the flight control centre with Estelle, Oriane and Solange to send me the following fax:

"You are always in our thoughts and part of us is flying with you… the wind is carrying you, carrying us, towards new horizons and we know that we will share life with you even more passionately after this adventure".

With tears in my eyes, I replied:

"I'm glad you came to have a look at the control centre on which I depend for this flight. The whole team takes it in turns to guide us, inform us, and even distract us during the night sometimes. I'm deeply grateful to you and the girls for your moral support; this is one of the most fascinating experiences in my life, but it's nothing compared to the love I feel for you. See you soon, I've got lots of things to tell you".

We were now 2,000 ft above the Indian rice fields and the architecture had changed. We could see some thatched roofs around the remains of a few Victorian buildings now colonised by vegetation. We no longer noticed the smells but the sounds of the area. The inversion layer in which we were still flying acted like an immense parabolic reflector amplifying everything: the folk music played in villages, car hooters, the noise made by craftsmen, but especially, and much to my delight, the shouts of children, of thousands of children, who greeted us noisily, happily surprised, along several hundred miles. Our arrival made every village come to a halt; people looked up, motionless, like colourful statues. Our silver tower couldn't go unnoticed, and if some hadn't looked up yet, our immense shadow informed them of an unusual presence. A woman wearing a long blue dress shyly raised an arm to greet us. A man used his mirror to send us a few luminous signals. Their mode of living was light years away from ours. With our technological monster, we were flying over whole regions whose people lived according to the rhythm of the sun and the monsoon, the growth of the rice and the birth of children. For them, time couldn't mean the same as for us westerners, and that may be why I identified with them during that dreamlike day; I dearly wished time would stop for me as well. I was sitting on the outer edge of the capsule. The balloon was perfectly balanced and slipped towards Calcutta without a sound. The country passed slowly by, I was deeply absorbed in my happiness, but also in my questioning. How could the inhabitants of a same planet have such different destinies? I wasn't ashamed of my happiness, but I was ashamed of all the suffering which I sensed beyond the horizon. I could feel the fragility, the precariousness of my state. What was the point of it all, of all the things I experienced or saw, of all the things I knew or ignored?

What was left of my scientific knowledge, of my philosophical convictions, of my boasting exclamations when I wondered about the meaning of life? Well, first of all, there were the answers, a load of answers. They were incomplete and trivial but reassuring, or at least they reassured me. They momentarily filled the gaps left by my uncertainties, enabling me to think as usual, strong from the validity of my mental reflexes. But I hadn't progressed a bit.

Then the question assailed me again, in a more insidious way. It grew inside me and I suddenly realised that my brain alone wouldn't provide the answer. Might it be easier to answer it with my heart? I let my feelings and emotions rise to the surface. All the misery in the world seemed even more appalling to me. I found it even more difficult to bear the unacceptable suffering, that unfair side of existence.

Beyond ideas, beyond emotions, the question remained, insistently, invading every cell in my body. I slowly understood that there was something else apart from my brain and my heart. As I considered the question and found no answer, a kind of new mysterious vibration overtook me; it made me feel fully alive.

The question had become as absolute as my self-awareness. The light changed a little; it became more precise, the colours more vivid, the sounds more definite. Curiously, my breathing had slowed down and went through me from head to foot, leaving me with an intense sensation of fullness. Perhaps that was what people called the Breath. I was fully aware of living inside my body and the question resounded in it like a new source of energy. I wished to God that no answer would materialise, that no conviction would seize me: it would make me lose at once that state of grace and enlightenment. I was carried by this mystery which not only opened onto the meaning of life but onto the very fact of existing at this precise moment.

I accepted to remain without the answer, I accepted to harbour some doubts, to let the unknown take over my inner world. I felt much better without certainties. In that state, it was easier to be following a trace in the sky without knowing where it would lead me to. That enormous question mark in the sky curiously opened new and unsuspected horizons for me.

But my intellect couldn't help nagging me:

'Right, you've got it: spirituality isn't an abstract concept, it's the full and absolute sensation of feeling that you exist. And the meaning of life is to open up to this miracle through the acceptance of doubt and the unknown; mystery, and mystery only, can provide this dimension of existence for you.'

The thought quickly turned into an answer, a new certainty, and the experience began to dissipate like a fragile veil torn by a storm. My sensation of existing disappeared and I was helpless about it. I was back to the realm of knowledge against my wish. All that remained was the distant memory of having lived something absolute for a while and the intense desire to find again the mystery of a question with no answer.

Soothed by the glow of sunset, next to the Plexiglas dome which was wide open, I felt that in such a place I could write a whole book. But I was brought back to the reality of our expedition. A moment before, which already seemed like a century ago, the pilot of the Swissair flight from Bangkok to Zurich had contacted me over the radio: he could see *Orbiter 2* undulating between rice fields. We had skimmed past the south of Calcutta and were already disappearing into the evening mist; and so was the poor air-traffic controller who was shouting himself hoarse trying to guide simultaneously twenty aeroplanes approaching our balloon: every five minutes he would ask for our position anxiously, yet it hardly changed at all.

We arrived over the Ganges delta by night, but the Moon offered us a fantastic show as we approached the sea: there was no coastline! The ponds widened while the expanses of land shrunk. It was impossible to know if the firm ground stretched into the ocean or if the ocean penetrated into the country. Every square inch seemed to be used up for the rice fields, well delimited by a fine protective edge. We couldn't understand how the farmers managed to find their way through such a maze of canals. The slightest storm, the slightest wave probably inundated the area with salt water... and famine.

Although there were several ports in the area, the ocean was totally deserted. As far as the eye could see, there wasn't a single light around. It was 82°F in the capsule and we still had the dome open. We'd made up our mind, we would cross the Bay of Bengal and head towards Burma... that's if the winds let us.

In the meantime, we received a fax informing us that the Chinese had just given a positive reply to the request we had made a year and a half ago... An hour earlier, Alan had officially announced the pending interruption of the expedition! The embassy of the People's Republic of China had sent these lines to the press:

"We are most interested in your attempt at doing a non-stop tour round the world. Having received a request from the Swiss government to allow you to overfly Chinese territory, the Chinese embassy in Bern immediately passed it on to the relevant Chinese authorities. After an urgent meeting, the authorities have informed, twenty-four hours before the flight over China was programmed, that the government has agreed to it. We hope that the next attempt by Mr Piccard and his team mates to do a trip round the world will be crowned with success".

As a journalist added later, jet streams don't wait for diplomats to make up their mind and they don't have the patience of the Orientals.

Nevertheless, the Chinese decision would be useful for the next attempt. I am grateful towards the Swiss government for backing up our project. I only hope that public opinion isn't going to unleash criticism against China. We must respect the differences of sensitivity and understand the Chinese reticence about some Occidentals coming to play with a balloon over their territory. They have other problems to deal with. Then a thought crossed my mind: what if it had been a round-the-world microlight flight planned by the Chinese? Would Switzerland have overlooked its ban on microlights? Certainly not...

During the night, the meteorologists expressed their preference for us to land in Myanmar, Burma's new name, rather than in Thailand. The winds wouldn't allow us to descend so far south and the Irrawady plain would be more welcoming than the mountainous jungle which stretches north of Bangkok. A private jet chartered from Geneva by Breitling had already left for Yangon with a retrieval team.

The adventure was coming to an end. We had less than thirty-six hours left, but I wanted to enjoy every minute of the flight before reaching the coast. During the past few days, the encounter with the earth, the fields and the men had been intense and fabulous. Now, we were over the open sea; the silvery waves which stretched as far as the eye could see reminded me of the

Chrysler Challenge. I like to fly over the oceans, their vast empty space becomes like a mirror. I had been following a trace in the sky for a long time and now felt closely linked to it. The music from my walkman was bringing back vivid memories, starting with Jonathan Livingston Seagull. Somehow, I felt nostalgic for hang gliding. This type of aerial dancing had opened a few secret doors and given me a better understanding of human beings. I recalled a scene shared with another pilot at the end of an air show: left alone to share our passion after the spectators had gone, we had formed a patrol – him with his microlight and me with my hang glider – to do a series of loops, wing to wing, lined up with the sunset but inverted, above a deserted airfield.

Moments like that give you the impression that life as a whole is beautiful and easy. It's often difficult to make allowances: if pleasure sometimes depends on illusion, Consciousness can only rest on truth. And now, I had the impression that truth was easier to reach when you are caught up in the breath of the wind over the ocean than under the applause of spectators watching you do aerobatics. I didn't disown anything, of course not, but the music of 'Let it be' coming from my earphones seemed to be more in tune with my new vision of life.

Let things be when you cannot change them, let the wind blow where it wants since you cannot stop it, and let the emotions of the moment rise to the surface. In one of his books, my grandfather hoped that after his stratospheric flights, which had opened up the way for modern aviation, the poetry and beauty of balloon flights wouldn't fall into oblivion. I must admit that there were few things I desired more at that instant than making our balloon win back the record of the longest flight in history; in memory of my grandfather's wish. Throughout the day I lived intensely every second of the eight hours which still separated me from that mythical record.

I knew that if I considered this record from my usual view-point, I would regard it as a source of pride and glory; but, there, half way across the Bay of Bengal, I saw it as a piece of Ariadne's thread. When the congratulations faxed by Richard Branson and Dick Rutan reached us on board, I started to cry with joy like a child. This was a historic moment for a loving grandson, and the most moving sunset of my life. I also remembered with gratitude Thedy Schneider with whom we had just written a few lines of the aeronautics epic: *Breitling Orbiter 2* had done the longest flight in the history of civil aviation. Thedy certainly deserved that record after making so many things possible for me.

The arrival in Myanmar was going to be difficult, as if we had to pay for that reward obtained after a long struggle. As soon as the night fell, the weather forecast became vague, and in complete contradiction with the observations we could make on the spot. I'd found a course which would take us to Yangon by dawn. Yet, in Geneva they told us to go upwards to reach the firm ground faster, even if that meant relying on coastal winds later to go further south.

We preferred to obey and took a fast layer which brought us between Ramree Island and the continent in two hours. We had the dome open because of the heat and could hear the purring of the burners which, added to the speed indicated by our GPS, gave us the impression of being in the cockpit of an airliner. In fact, we reached the Burmese territory far too soon. Darkness prevented us from seeing the Arakan Yoma mountain range which overlooked the sea, and the coastal winds were blowing in all directions. Below us, a few fishermen sent some light signals from their huts. What must they have thought? We replied to them by firing the propane burners. We descended as much as possible to try and avoid the mountains, but the airstreams that pushed us were unstoppable. If we went back up, we would arrive too soon and too far north in the Irrawady valley, and none of us wanted to risk a night landing. There was only one thing left: crossing the Arakan Yoma keeping close to its summits to fly slowly without being dragged towards the north. The flight control centre tried to dissuade us, but it was the only solution.

It was my turn to rest for a few hours. In the meantime, Andy hopped over the mountains as planned, while Wim scrutinised the shadows to help him with his observations. The control centre didn't understand our manoeuvre. Andy got so annoyed that he unplugged the fax and the telephone, causing panic in Geneva.

I didn't want to sleep for too long; I preferred directing the operations and discovering the landscape that unveiled itself before us at dawn. The mountains were just a bad memory now. I connected our communication instruments again and apologised on behalf of Andy. The three of us watched the arrival over the immense Irrawady River; several watercourses meandered in parallel and mirrored the pinkish light of the welcoming dawn. The wind soundings gave us room for manoeuvre to try and reach the only road in the valley.

In Geneva, they hadn't taken our flight strategy seriously and warned Yangon too late. They woke up and startled the retrieval team:

"*Orbiter 2* will be landing in Minhla in 19 minutes!"

It was action stations for the team and for the journalists, who rushed to the taxis and the helicopter hired from the army. They had known nothing but stress during the previous days. In just a few hours, they'd had to get air tickets for flights which were already fully booked and entry visas to a country which normally refused access to the press. It was the Myanmar ambassador in Paris, himself a pilot and fascinated with our expedition, who had seen to all the necessary procedures. But nothing would have been possible on the spot without an intervention from Max-O. Wey, the Yangon delegate of the marvellous François-Xavier Bagnoud Association, which puts all its energies into helping wounded children.

I didn't want to put our landing at risk just to wait for the helicopter, but we still tried to hold on in the air a bit more. The weak winds close to the ground made it possible. The conditions were ideal, but my heart was heavy despite all the excitement. Andy had raised the solar panels but our telephone aerial still worked:

"Geneva, from *Breitling Orbiter 2*, we will be landing in 10 minutes. All is well, but no helicopter in sight".

On the road, some dumbfounded people gathered to watch this mysterious apparition. Some of them bowed down. Later, one of them told a journalist: "I thought it was a monk in levitation in a flying pagoda". True enough, that little house hanging under the silver cloud might have had the saffron colour of the buddhist monk's robe from a distance!

The enormous shadow of the balloon stroked several glittering pagodas. Andy controlled the burners, I controlled the valve and Wim checked the altitude from the rear porthole. The field in front of us was ideal, it contained no obstacles and was cut by a lane. I opened the valve and our precious helium began to mix with the Burmese atmosphere. Andy unrolled the guide rope and fired the burners once or twice to slow the descent. The capsule landed delicately over the dust without a single jolt. A that very moment, the helicopter arrived, as if a miraculous meeting had been planned 5,000 miles apart. Simultaneously, a military lorry belted down to reach us amidst a cloud of dust. Some soldiers jumped out and cordoned off the balloon to keep the crowd away.

I climbed down the ladder with the same emotion as when I had climbed up it ten days earlier. Ten days in that capsule which I now watched from the outside; ten days of dreaming, or more precisely 233 hours and 55 minutes, although we were in Myanmar rather than back to the starting point. We didn't manage to do a complete revolution, but I didn't want to tarnish the images that were deep inside me or spoil them with deception and bitterness.

Alan arrived and I fell into his arms. The last time had been in Montpellier, after the sea landing.

"This place is prettier!"

"You've had a marvellous flight!"

It was strange to find part of our team in the middle of nowhere: Monika, Stephano, Brian, and several faithful journalists had crossed the world to see us land. They had been following my adventures in the air for so long that they had become my friends.

When I saw our immense balloon neatly parked in that bean field, I felt both relieved and sad. I wanted to laugh and cry at the same time. But the local weather forecast didn't give us time, the wind and the first morning thermals already shook our envelope. The size of the rip panel was too small. The heat dilated the helium faster than it could escape through the valve and the balloon began to get inflated again. An officer shot at the fabric with a Kalashnikov, to no avail. I was horrified, we would have to destroy the envelope to save the capsule. Since the machine-gun hadn't given any result, we tried to open the helium cell with our Swiss knives; that was useless, the wind grew stronger and rushed into the balloon which turned into a giant spinnaker. We feared we would lose the envelope if we detached it, so we only freed three out of the four anchoring devices. The wind flattened it onto the dusty ground, leaving it partly torn. The natives then understood that they would have a feast trying to help us. It was the kill, the quarry. In ten minutes, the envelope was lacerated, torn in strips of a few yards each. The whole crowd had a go at it; a man was even cycling inside the envelope when the wind suddenly straightened part of the balloon. The soldiers, whose attitude was no longer threatening, decided not to intervene. Most parts and pieces were recovered and sorted out but a certain quantity vanished into thin air. A few houses would soon have some silvery curtains and would be cooled by aeronautical ventilators working with solar panels! A futuristic city had just been founded in Myanmar…

Then I was able to call Michèle via satellite to reassure her:

"I have so many things to tell you. I feel like going home to be able to spend some time with my family at last".

I imagined her smile as she replied:

"Knowing you, my love, you'll probably write a book when you get home!"

I was sitting in the middle of the field. A big circle of onlookers had formed around me, it was the first time these natives met white foreigners. They couldn't quite understand why I was speaking through a telephone apparently not connected to anything. I would have liked to establish a more personal contact with them, but they were frightened of these men who had come from the sky. All I could do was clasp my hands over my heart and incline my head slightly to do the Buddhist greeting, which means: I bow before the divine part in you. They looked amused and greeted me back the same way.

Alan interrupted my attempt at establishing a dialogue and pushed me into the helicopter which had to take us back to the capital city. I would have like to stay a bit more in Oke Kwin, where our capsule now looked like a time machine. Unfortunately, we were already expected at a press conference in Yangon and had to quickly legalise our presence on Burmese territory. The country had been subjected to decades of nationalist dictatorship and we were probably the first foreigners to enter it without a visa. We were not going to be able to meet Aung San Suu Kyi, the dissident democrat under home arrest; but at least we had shown that country, withdrawn into itself, that Occidentals don't only bring imperialism and pollution. In fact, with its usual good manners, Breitling had already indemnified the owner of the bean field which had been trampled by the crowd.

My heart was still in Oke Kwin and I wanted to escape from formality and society gossip. Barefoot in Shwedagon alleys, I could now fully enjoy the physical contact with the country in which I had landed. Plexiglas and aerials had given way to domes and turrets, which glowed with the same golden light when the last rays of the sun were setting over Yangon. At last I could escape and find a moment of serenity among hundreds of statues of Buddha which guarded the largest pagoda in the world. The style had less frills than Thai art and I appreciated the purity of its lines. I was happy to recharge my batteries in that peaceful place reserved for prayer, and trod each tile of the sacred floor with respect.

I could feel that my social life was going to change, because even here some unknown tourists already asked me for an autograph. Not that I was looking for fame, but I was glad that so many people had wished to share my dream. I needed some silence; I needed to express my gratitude for having had such a fascinating life so far.

However, I didn't understand why I had landed in Myanmar after lifting off to do a trip round the Earth. What was I meant to do in that country? What was I meant to learn there? Even if the press had devoted its front page to it, the arrival of my balloon wasn't likely to revolutionise local politics. I let myself be guided, secretly wondering which synchronicity would provide me with an explanation. I ended up in an antique shop, like in Shanghai before the Chrysler Challenge. I started looking for something, unconsciously, examining every item, but didn't find anything. Suddenly, the shopkeeper brought me another object as I was already on the way out.

184

It was an engraved silver vase, representing Bodhisattvas in meditation, with their hands clasped over their heart and their head slightly inclined. On the lid, a monk appeared to be dancing. A medallion bore a few volutes containing characters which I couldn't decipher.

The shopkeeper noticed I was examining it:

"Do you want to know what it says?"

"Yes."

I was shaking a little.

"Welcome to the newcomer".

So, there was nothing to understand? Just something to accept?

I turned towards my guide inquisitively:

"Is that all?"

"That's how the shopkeeper translated it."

"And how would you translate it?"

"It's difficult…"

"Please, try".

"It says… May the spiritual… and the human worlds… harvest the fruits… of great achievements…"

"…"

"You're looking pensive".

WINDS OF HOPE

Our only freedom is to change altitude

INDEED, I WAS PENSIVE, and remained so for a long while, pondering over that Burmese maxim which I didn't understand. What could I do with it? What great achievement was it referring to? Not my flight, obviously! Although it had been a fascinating experience on a personal level, it was nonetheless a bitter failure for a round-the-world attempt.

Again, this was a question with no answer which I had to consider with all my heart. With total honesty and without prejudice. How could I get a better understanding of how the wind blows? I had learnt about concentration, achievement and even a certain type of consciousness through my struggle with the elements, while flying into the wind. Then it had occurred to me that my potential could be stimulated even further if I stopped insisting on having everything under control. But I had just landed in the middle of nowhere, in a sea of doubts. A thought crossed my mind: what if I was on the wrong trace? What if this adventure wasn't meant for me? Was it possible, was it even reasonable to try going round the world with the wind? Was my new alliance with nature really going to take me anywhere? The victory of the Chrysler Challenge suddenly seemed so far away... 'Beginner's luck?' as Paolo Coelho, author of The Alchemist, would have said.

Then, during the following weeks, I had the growing impression that I was grappling with life itself as much as with a trip around the world. Exactly as in that marvellous petition by Roman emperor Marcus Aurelius learnt in my school days:

'Give me the strength to change what I can, the courage to accept what I cannot change, and the wisdom to distinguish the difference between the two.'

In the past, that sentence had struck me as a little abstract, as somewhat difficult to apply. But after the recent events, it gradually became obvious because it reflected what I had felt throughout my last flight.

It was clear that a balloon moves with the wind, depending on the direction imposed by nature, which it cannot control. Isn't man also in a helpless situation when caught up in the winds of life? He feels pushed by events, trapped in his problems, his convictions and his personal vision of the world. Health, like illness and accidents, love or failure, wealth, crises, luck or ruin, are all like the wind. Everything in life takes us by surprise and pushes us towards the unknown. And here is our biggest problem: we hate the unknown…

Our education, our culture, our society, teach us to focus on certainties, to apply principles, to fight against doubt, to avoid questions with no answers, instead of teaching us to make the most of what we may learn from life. We try to develop knowledge, not experience. As a result, our first reaction, of course, is to try and keep things under control constantly. To fight against the winds of life… we sometimes do it quite successfully, but only too rarely. Many trying tests escape our control, and the feeling of impotence they produce on us can increase our suffering, our pain and our despair even more.

Then what freedom do we have in life? Well, exactly the same as the pilot of a balloon. By changing his flight level, by exploring the sky vertically, the aeronaut discovers that the atmosphere is made of various air layers, which all travel in different directions and at different speeds. To find a better flight path, all the pilot can do is change his altitude. As human beings, this is what we should learn to do with our life, on a psychological, philosophical and even spiritual level, if we want to find other currents, other influences, other ways of understanding and living our lives. Yes, the only true freedom we have in life is our capacity to 'change altitude'.

This means that we must agree to question ourselves, to alter our repetitive patterns of thoughts and behaviour; to open up to other ideas which can change our perception; to stop wanting to convince others that we are in the right; to listen to them and respect their differences so as to learn what they can teach us. To change altitude also means to be prepared to do exactly the opposite of what we've always done so far.

I remember that I once asked a bilingual friend for the English translation of 'se remettre en question' and that he replied with total conviction:

'There is no term for it in English, and that's just as well, the French language shouldn't have one either! You should never "question yourself", you should go for things straight away, without thinking, or else you'll never reach your goals!'

It's easy to suggest an analogy between a balloon and life itself, or to say that our whole life is like a flight in a balloon and that we only have to change our view of the world, to question ourselves, in order to find the best course and change our destiny. Unfortunately, it is a lot more difficult to put it all into practice. When you are in a balloon, before you can change altitude you have to lighten its weight, to dump ballast. In life, you have to do the same, except that the ballast we dispose of is precisely what we have been told to keep like a precious treasure. I am talking about our certainties and other convictions, our paradigms and well-established dogmas, the habits and automatic reflexes which make us react rather than act, the definitions behind which we seek refuge to avoid doubts or the unknown. We think they make us feel stronger and more efficient. But, that's wrong. They make us more static, rigid, unable to change, to adapt, to evolve.

When we give priority to possessing, controlling, satisfying immediate impulses, when all we do is react according to our habits and automatic reflexes, we expose ourselves to the turbulence of life, which will sweep us like mere grains of dust. Changing altitude consists in developing our inner freedom, liberating ourselves from our deep-rooted fear of the unknown, from the illusion that we can decide on the direction of the wind; it consists in opening up to the meaning of terrestrial life, to look for the best way of Being rather than Having, without indulgence, to feel deep inside us that we exist, advancing step by step on the path which leads to the Essence.

There was no way I was going to stop my exploration of life; the trip round the world became a new symbol of it. I could foresee a third attempt as the means to continue following a trace in the sky, as I had been doing for a long while.

However, in order to succeed we also had to change altitude in our project, i.e. to challenge ourselves very specifically in relation to our plans and strategies. There was no question of us embarking again on a fast flight with jet streams; it didn't give us enough leeway to try and avoid political, geographical or meteorological obstacles. We therefore needed a different balloon. We needed one which could make use of all the atmospheric layers without consuming more gas. And, especially, one which could wait at a low altitude, without endangering our flight autonomy, until the highest airstreams took the right course. In the end, we had to build a new capsule with burners that worked with propane rather than kerosene, and a different envelope, with improved insulation. The old material was thrown like ballast... into a museum!

We also had to find a co-pilot whose personality fitted in with the necessary challenges, and I must admit that it was difficult. This time the team had made it clear to me that my debt to Wim was paid off and that I had to find another co-pilot. For a few months, I considered choosing a Concorde flight engineer, but that was a flop. Twenty-five years of service in front of the same instruments in the same cockpit hadn't turned him into a pioneer seeking innovation… he felt out of step before our very experimental construction, he was too set in his ways and had to give up the project. Of course, the press made fun of this problem, insisting more on the relational conflict than on the absolute need for us to form a totally reliable team. Some Swiss journalists even openly sided with competing teams. But that was the least of my worries!

Nobody had thought of Brian Jones as a co-pilot, he was so perfect in the role of technician at the flight control centre. Yet, he emerged as the most suitable candidate, not through his insistence, but because of his flexibility and his human qualities within the team. A few months before, he had offered to be our reserve pilot. He knew that after undergoing full training he would probably remain on the firm ground and watch us lift off with disappointment, but had accepted that and it had placed him in the right place, at the right time. What a magnificent example for all those who never undertake anything for fear of failure.

In fact, I knew Brian very little and suggested we develop our relationship through the communication techniques I had learnt. The main thing was to avoid the usual traps in this kind of situation.

Normally, when we come into contact with people, we tend to unconsciously project onto them our expectations and our fears but also everything we reckon they might be or think. Since we are afraid of differences, we like to think others are like us, we don't see them as they really are. And if we can't imagine them being like us, we reject them, not for what they are but for what we reckon they are.

In our case, there was a serious risk of mutual idealisation; I was afraid of not finding the right co-pilot, Brian was only too happy to get his chance to fly at last. We could end up having the wrong idea of each other, seeing things in a distorted manner. The gap between reality and projections would then gradually deepen and give way to severe disillusion. With the passing of time or because of stress, our true personality would eventually be perceived through unexpected reactions or attitudes. In cases like that, it is typical to accuse others of having changed or having betrayed our trust and dissimulated their true nature, when in fact we hadn't seen them as they really were. Unfortunately, this is how many marriages and social, friendly or professional relationships are built and destroyed.

The plan for our preparation consisted in getting to know each other by underlining one another's differences, without paying much attention to our supposed similarities. We looked for the differences in our past lives, the differences in our experiences, the differences in our vision of life, of the world, the differences in our personalities, our nature, our reactions. If we were alike, there would be no advantage whatsoever in flying together rather than alone. We use a battery for its different potentials. Once both poles are identical we throw it away because it can no longer provide us with the energy we need.

Then why be afraid of exploiting the differences in human polarities? It must be because we don't know how to make them complementary, how to make them work in synergy. We frequently reject other people's ideas during exchanges based on the pursuit of power and control. We try to prove we're right and end up shattering the trust and creativity of others. The relationship can only end in an equation where $1 + 1 = 0$.

The teams who aim to step out of this pattern, to avoid differences of opinion and conflicts, may then fall into the trap which consists of gathering only people who are very similar. This cancels all creativity since there is no added value; everyone shares the same ideas. In this type of relationship, 1 + 1 only equals 1.

Of course, 1 + 1 can also equal 2. For example, if there is little interaction between the partners, each sticking to their own ideas, differences are not threatening. But there is no synergy.

Brian and I therefore spoke a lot about our respective lives, trying to explain why we thought we had become what we were. We learned to understand the respective paths which had led us to where we were: it was the only way of accepting the other as he was, rather than expecting him to do things which he couldn't do. This attitude doesn't aim at avoiding conflicts, which are often a source of new ideas, but of developing the means to solve them. With this mode of communication, the other person doesn't feel attacked by your observations and accepts your criticism without being offended. The idea is to express yourself on the basis of your own feelings, without trying to change others. There is a great difference between saying 'this situation makes me feel uncomfortable' and 'stop behaving like this'.

We managed to create a type of communication whereby partners, being as different from one another as possible, still shared a basic value: we wanted to understand what others could bring us, rather than insist on teaching them what we knew. Given that people can only be the result of the experiences they have gone through during their life, we should always try to understand why they think the way they do, rather than focus on what they say or try to change them.

The result is a relationship in which 1 + 1 = 3! In our case, there was Brian, me, and the both of us. It was the same with the meteorologists, Pierre Eckert, Luc Truellemans, and the two of them; and so forth and so on for the rest of the team.

This technique is limited because it requires a great deal of honesty, with others but also with yourself. If it gets twisted, it allows you to gain power over your interlocutor and destroy the relationship to your own advantage.

In the end, it was like a game despite the difficulty at stake: we had to regard communication as a means of comparing experiences rather than sharing ideas or facts. If you limit yourself to exchanging facts, opinions or ideas, you enter a limited process which leaves out all the reasons why people get to where they are. On the contrary, comparing an experience means realising that there are many ways of going through the same events; it means understanding that there are countless ways of solving the same problem, that we often use identical words to describe different things, or different words to describe identical things. To compare an experience, means to walk in someone else's shoes for a while, to discover a new vision of the world. It's a way of 'changing altitude' within the relationship, to face the numerous facets of reality which we often believe to be unique. In a team, that means you can combine every member's strategies to end up inventing an entirely new one. Like in a symbolic flight in a balloon, you have to follow the energy of the other members rather than try to go against it and control it.

Funnily enough, our competitors never understood why we had decided to have two meteorologists. They probably found it unnecessary, not being familiar with the equation $1+1 = 3$. The result was drastic: every time their sole meteorologist made a mistake, their flight came to a premature halt.

The training of the team had shown that respect and honesty were not idealistic or out-of-date notions, but very efficient relational aids. We now had to use them outside the team, and especially with the Chinese authorities, who still hadn't given us their authorisation for the next attempt.

We therefore decided to go to China to negotiate. In every meeting, human relations seemed like a game with the wind rather than against it.

Our competitors were still applying for an authorisation via their own country, as we had been doing until then, using the argument that all other countries had given us the go ahead. For them, it proved that there was no problem in entering any air space in a balloon. This was going against the wind, against the experience of our interlocutors, who couldn't change their position without losing face. When we landed in Peking, we used a different approach. We had understood at last that it was wiser to proceed the other way round. We started by apologising to the Chinese officials for causing them so many problems. We put ourselves in their place. It became clear that their refusal stemmed from the difficulty for their country, ill-equipped with radar systems, to control the passage of a balloon over its immense territory. We therefore had to consider their problems and try to find a solution together. Our attitude changed the relationship completely, it was no longer based on a power struggle. They confessed that our team was the only one to have shown respect and consideration for them. In that frame of mind, they were going to do everything they could to help us get what we needed from the 'relevant authorities', the army. And so they did. However, to avoid getting into an awkward position with other countries, they gave the same authorisation to all competitors.

We had to use the same strategy in December 1998, when Richard Branson and Steve Fossett, flying in the same balloon, crossed the centre of China although it had been specifically excluded from the authorisation. Furious, the Chinese cancelled their authorisation to all competitors still on the firm ground.

Rather than being indignant and trying to prove it had nothing to do with me, I immediately replied:

'I am very sorry about the incident. Be assured that I won't lift off for a third attempt before getting a new authorisation from you.'

The Chinese ambassador immediately invited me to embark on new negotiations, and I ended up recovering the right to overfly that country. But I was the only one, which represented a significant advantage for my team.

In the meantime, the international race was hotting up, and the number of competitors increased. We felt a little overpowered by the English and American millionaires' propaganda. But not being the most powerful encourages you to be the most creative. Undoubtedly, the changes we had introduced made us feel that we now had the best balloon and the best team. Most of our competitors, on their side, had learnt very little from their mistakes, and continued to fail in every attempt for the same reasons.

After our success, many journalists asked me how we'd managed to defeat such major competitors. In fact, all we had done was adopt the strategy of the wasp, rather than imitate that of the bee. I had observed on several occasions that bees always got trapped in the covered terrace where my family took its summer meals. They were unable to change strategy, they struggled on and on against the first glass panel they met and thought they could reach freedom because they saw it on the other side. They eventually died of exhaustion without ever understanding their error. Wasps, on the contrary, first caught a bit of food off the table, and if they hit themselves against a pane of glass they tried all the rest until they found their way out. I had often used this amusing example to teach my children the difference between fierceness and perseverance.

Several teams never took off, due to technical or political problems. Steve Fossett was stopped once again by a stormy front, since he didn't have a pressurised capsule which would have allowed him to avoid the obstacle. He even saw his envelope being torn off by turbulence from a storm cloud and rocket down into the Pacific. Richard Branson did an emergency sea landing in Hawaii with a balloon which still lacked the correct thermal insulation, something which affected its flight autonomy. Andy Elson, who had set up his own project and had managed to avoid China from the south, which was quite an exploit, had to stop in the Sea of Japan because of the same type of technical errors he had made in the design of *Orbiter 1* and *Orbiter 2*.

As for us, we avoided boasting. We had to wait for such a long time for the right meteorological window that we didn't leave Château-d'Œx until 1st March 1999, at the very end of the jet stream season. Few people still believed in the success of our enterprise and criticism had arrived from all directions. It had been agreed with Breitling that this would be our last attempt, our last chance to succeed.

On a technical level, the first ten days of the flight were going to be decisive. The permit obtained from the Chinese authorities was of crucial importance but it was limited to the southern strip of the country. In order to observe its terms, we first had to go from Switzerland to North Africa and catch the subtropical jet stream to arrive in Asia south of the 26th parallel. In order to achieve this we had to skirt anti-clockwise around an area of low pressure in the Mediterranean. Originally, we had planned to fly in a straight line, this now meant a 6 day-detour over the Sahara and an extra 6,000 miles. Enough to leave us short of fuel well before the end of the tour, which was due to last 15 days and cover under 22,000 miles.

However, when you are at the mercy of the wind, plans become irrelevant; what you need is flexibility and a capacity to adapt. If we had stuck to the first criteria for our project, we would never have lifted off. We had to risk a third failure to be in a position to reach victory. Paradoxically, it was thanks to the Chinese restrictions that our success was so complete. Because we had to use a path that went so far south, we avoided all the storms which would have blocked us in the north of the Pacific. Thanks to the enormous and worrying detour we made via Africa, our flight became the longest in the history of aviation, both in terms of distance and duration. It just proves that some of life's most beautiful gifts can be wrapped up in ugly paper tied with tatty string. The parcel makes the problem look insuperable, yet it contains solutions nobody would ever have thought of. Far removed from the feats covered by the media, the spirit of adventure consists in opening the unexpected parcels which life brings you, rather than rejecting them because you haven't ordered them. It's a bit worrying to see that through our need to control everything we struggle to stick to a chosen course when the winds of life offer us a different one. The hardest thing is to know when you have to struggle or when you should go along with what life gives you.

Of course, when we lifted off, we couldn't have known that this endless detour which lengthened our flight so much contained the seed of our major success. We were worried in case we failed. But what would we achieve in life if we refrained from doing things every time we're afraid! Throughout the first day, while we flew over the Alps, I kept on thinking that adventurers and explorers are just as frightened as anyone else, the only difference is that they go ahead with their projects all the same! So, it may be that to explore life we need perseverance, more than courage.

I will not come back to all the flight details which Brian and I already related in *The Greatest Adventure (UK) or in Around the world in 20 days (USA)*. However, I would like to recreate in the next few pages that mixture of doubt and hope, fear and trust, clouds and wind, as true as life itself, which pervaded the atmosphere of our biggest and dearest dream. I would like to recreate that marvellous impression of being part of nature, of belonging to the planet, of embracing the world. Advancing always in the same direction, we finally came back to the starting point... and would never be the same again. We lived in the sky for 20 days and 20 nights. We watched the planet breathe to the rhythm of the elements, the rhythm of the clouds which were born at dawn and died at dusk. For three weeks we saw colours and reflections change constantly from sunrise to sunset.

At the end of each night, a very fine clear line would separate the sky from the earth. Then it would grow thicker until the whole sky became silvery above the Earth still black. And suddenly, in a flash, the red sun would splash the world with its light and make it come back to life. The mountains, the plains, the deserts or the oceans then appeared, putting a face on the geographical data indicated by our GPS, every morning was different, little by little we were slowly advancing in proportion to the globe, heading for an invisible, unattainable finish, pushed by the winds of hope.

Every night, we were surrounded by stars, floating silently in the universe. In order to fully absorb the infinity of the cosmos, we often switched off the lights in the cockpit, to see a few more galaxies over there, far away in that immense emptiness which filled us. As far as we knew, those billions of stars didn't light up any life despite their brightness, but when our sun rose in the middle of the horizon, life suddenly appeared before us with all its magic, and the miracle of its uniqueness. We couldn't understand how mankind can live on the only inhabited planet in the Milky Way without perceiving the miraculous side of it; without being able to establish an intimate relationship with the Earth, based on affection and respect. The word respect was taking on a greater meaning as the days went by. Respect, in the sense of learning to recognise the spark of this magical life which all beings, whether human or not, carry inside them, and which should make us change our attitude towards them. The inner feeling that the spark which animates every being in the world was deeply related to ours called for respect. Our intensified sensation of existing, as if we suddenly perceived our soul, fell in harmony with the existence of our environment, and allowed us to become a full part of it.

And yet, in the meantime, how much horror, how many atrocities were taking place down below? There was famine in the Sahel with the dreadful disease and poverty that it implied. There were civil wars and loathsome prisons in so many countries. There were the innocent victims of conflicts launched across the globe to serve particular interests. The more I contemplated the beauty of the world, the less I could ignore the horror and suffering which tore it apart; that permanent suffering which won't go away even though we stop thinking about it. Every day, our flight was becoming a more accessible dream while the people below didn't even have the means to save their children from dying. We couldn't just close our eyes. I remember that Brian and I spoke more and more about what went on below our superb balloon. What a contrast between the crude reality of the world and our desire, almost naïve, to go around it! Obviously, we ended up talking of what we would do with the one-million dollar cheque which we would get from Budweiser if we completed the journey around the earth. The conditions stipulated that half of that prize was to go to a humanitarian organisation. That would be a way of redistributing the extraordinary luck we'd had in being born on the right side of the barrier, away from the horror of those regions where the cries of children in pain ought to prevent the whole world from going to sleep at night.

As in the Burmese maxim, which suddenly took on some meaning, the human world could then harvest some of the fruits of our achievement. But we were so far from it that we hardly dared mention it. There were still many obstacles to overcome before that hypothetical victory could materialise.

We couldn't even progress at the desired speed. We had to content ourselves with what nature had decided. Our meteorologists called us again when we were above the Sahara. It was the fourth day of the flight and we had acquired a speed of 75 mph, when in fact Luc and Pierre had only planned half of that. To tease them, I told them over the satellite telephone:

"Have you seen what great pilots we are? We're flying twice as fast as you thought we were!"

The reply came back as a cold shower:

"Nobody asked you to fly that fast. You've got to get down at least 3000 ft to slow down!"

"Why slow down? We still have 25,000 miles to cover. We can't keep on dragging ourselves over the desert wasting our fuel away…"

"You may be in a hurry, but you're flying at an altitude at which the winds will back and will take you to the North Pole".

Then, after a short pause, they continued almost ironically.

"Hey, you the good pilots up there, do you want to head quickly in the wrong direction… or slowly in the right one?"

Meteorologists are essential, and not only when it comes to guiding balloons. They should be everywhere, in politics, in businesses, in schools. They should teach us the value of long-term decisions in a society based on profit and immediate satisfaction which is heading towards a dead end at top speed. They would help us to form an alliance with the winds of Life to make better use of them.

Admittedly, when you are 28,000 ft above the Sahara, consumed with the hope of fulfilling your dream at last, it isn't easy to change altitude and slow down. But it was obvious that our success depended on Nature, not on our own will. We had to progress at exactly the same speed as the depression over the Mediterranean, now pushing us eastwards. The idea was to reach an area of high pressure centred over India to then enter Chinese territory to the south of the 26th parallel, which defined the authorised corridor.

However, we didn't intend to just be pushed haphazardly. Quite the other way round. We had to stabilise our enormous balloon within a layer which was going at the right speed and in the right direction. That required much concentration at all times because of the inertia of the 810,000-cubic feet envelope. There was no room for fatalism, we weren't going to give up the tiny amount of control we had. But there was no room for stress either, i.e. the exhausting habit of struggling against things over which you have no control.

After crossing India and China in a powerful jet stream going at around 95 mph, our speed came right down to 15 mph over the Pacific, and there was nothing we could do but accept it. We had to accept trailing across the largest ocean of the planet, with the risk of running out of fuel and landing on the sea before we reached America, which would mean riding some 30 ft waves for several days until a boat came to our rescue. We had to accept losing all computer transmissions from Geneva for 48 hours, we had to accept our anguish…

And the anguish grew as we tried to counter it. But, if we accepted it deep down, if we let it play its role and spoke about it together, it gradually disappeared and we let ourselves be pushed very slowly to the other shore. So many problems in ordinary life come from the refusal to suffer, and from all the strategies we set up to avoid the reality of life. Up there, you couldn't deceive yourself or your team mate before that merciless mirror which reflected the whole of your emotions. After the launching of the project, the humiliation of the failures, the criticism about my strategy, the patience and the perseverance which made us start again despite of it all, I had got to the most frightening stage of this (almost) initiatory flight: the crossing of the abyss. I had reached a breaking point from which I might find the strength to continue.

When we did the night watch, alone in the cold atmosphere of the cockpit, we only had the onboard camera to talk to. I sometimes spoke to it as if it were the last witness to see me alive, totally oblivious of what people would think if they saw the film – supposing we came back. I no longer took the outer world into consideration; I simply felt that I had become genuine. Deep down, I knew it would be impossible to complete this trip round the world without divine help; or superior help if you prefer. I had done everything in my power to get there, but the rest was beyond my scope.

The balloon, much lighter after burning 4,500 lb of liquid propane in 12 days, had now stabilised itself at 30,000 ft. We had to wait for 5 ¼ days at very low speed before being taken care of *in extremis* by a powerful jet stream, which Pierre and Luc had expected over that area of the Pacific. In just forty-eight hours we were able to cross the other half of the ocean at 112 mph and arrive above Mexico.

That's when the crossing of the abyss turned to despair... All the forecasts had given us reasons to hope for an easy end, but the main current threw us out towards Latin America. It was the 17th day of the flight, and what remained of our physical and mental strength was going to be put to the test. That path led us south-wards and we were helpless, worn out by nervous tension, half asphyxiated, probably because of a mistake in the gas mixture of the capsule, frozen because of a breakdown in the heating system, in tears at the thought of seeing our dream shatter.

Several friends, who had either ascended Everest, gone round the world in an aeroplane or landed on the moon, had told me similar stories. It was just before the final victory that the biggest crisis took place. Later, I wondered if it wasn't one more test which life had put us through to check that we weren't giving up, that we were worthy of a victory.

The last manoeuvre to be attempted was the exploration of all the layers of the atmosphere in order to find the best wind. Exactly as in life, in fact, where you can only solve a crisis by exploring all the possible altitudes, i.e. all the fathomable solutions, strategies and behaviours, rather than insist on the same course of action over and over again. We sacrificed a huge amount of propane to gradually reach the maximum altitude our balloon could manage that day: 34,600 ft. I couldn't take my eyes off the GPS which still indicated a southern course. It was only in the last 300 ft, when we seemed to have lost our bet, that the wind turned miraculously towards Africa.

Our path seemed safe, but the speed had come right down to 30 mph. We still had some 6,000 miles to cover, with only 4 propane cylinders out of 32. This meant a quarter of the planet, with an eighth of the fuel supply. The figures obviously pointed to the end of the adventure, but we didn't recognise their authority. We felt as if we no longer belonged to that world. This was something different. We were suddenly taken over by an incredible force which had arisen inside us, which had taken its source among our deepest fears, and which would make us fly until the last drop of propane, wherever that took us. Giving up was not a valid option. Indeed, our strategy began to bear its fruits and enabled us to take that risk. By leaving from Switzerland and coming back towards Mauritania, we had pushed back the fictitious finish westwards. And since we had avoided lifting off from the United States, we could land over the Atlantic in case of an emergency, rather than over the Pacific, which was more cruel. The Atlantic… Was it going to welcome me again, or had it given me all it could during the Chrysler Challenge? After all, what did it matter since Brian and I had decided to continue, come what may?

And then, suddenly, all the obstacles vanished in one go. In a few hours, our speed went from 30 to 120 mph. The insurmountable barriers of cumulo-nimbus which our team had spotted by satellite disappeared, and, against all odds, the American air-traffic controllers authorised us to cross their airways to go across the ocean. Two days later, we were in Mauritania. We had a few hours left before passing the last meridian. A few hours before having changed forever. These were the longest hours in my life…

We were both in the cockpit, watching the GPS data come out on our computers. In Geneva, everybody was restless. Satellite dishes from all televisions in the world had taken the PC by storm. Alan Noble, our chief of mission, was savouring with the whole team the last moments which still separated us from a total victory.

'Don't gloat, seemed to whisper the burners as they died out an hour before we got to the finish; this victory has nothing to do with you. It has to do with your destiny; it is up to you to do something with it. Success is measured in terms of what you give, not in terms of what you get…'

It took us several minutes to light them again and recover our altitude. Those minutes were enough for us to understand that we were not the heroes of this adventure. Something else, borne by the winds of hope, had allowed our balloon to make a journey around life without an engine or a rudder… Brian and I called this 'something else' the Invisible Hand (but you can call it what you like) with a feeling of belonging to a Whole which transcended us.

Some people, who don't understand how badly our society needs to go back to its spiritual roots, were offended by our statements. How could the heir of a dynasty of scientists end up making such irrational references? They preferred to imagine that the physical and the spiritual worlds are totally separate from one another. Nevertheless, they still complained about life having no apparent meaning.

The last meridian was now behind us. We had fallen into each other's arms and were still holding one another by the shoulders, savouring the instant we had been waiting for so long. Our impossible dream had come true, we had succeeded, but we couldn't believe it. In any case, the true celebrations could only begin once we were reunited with our team on the firm ground.

A journey had come to an end, but another was about to start. Our balloon, lighter by almost its entire fuel supply, was now flying at 140 mph, 38,000 ft above the Sahara, hoping to make a safe landing in the Egyptian sand. A cheque with many zeros was waiting for us 'to make the human world harvest the fruits of our achievement'. A very fine crescent Moon had risen exactly in front of us. We were free of any tension. Far from feeling empty after so many efforts, we felt profoundly happy and grateful to life. For the first time, we could seriously talk about what we would do with that prize without making mere assumptions.

That was when our humanitarian foundation was born, between the Earth and the Sky. Rather than distributing the money to charity organisations, all of a sudden and without any real consequences, we thought of using it for a long term project to help those whose situation was far removed from ours. The aim would be to fight against the suffering of the forgotten or neglected children who lived in areas we had overflown, and who didn't have the opportunity to see their most basic dream, such as surviving misery and indifference, come true.

Our first step would be to fight against noma, a disease clearly related to poverty. We would use the interest from the Budweiser prize, together with the financial and media spin-offs of our success, in the form of public or private donations, interviews or political meetings. Every year, as a result of hunger and lack of hygiene, 100,000 children from the poorest countries in the world suffer horrendous facial deformity because of this scourge.

Malnutrition makes them prone to gingivitis and weakens their defences, causing a necrotising infection against which their organism cannot fight back and which attacks the surrounding tissue, often destroying their face completely. However, if the disease is checked in time it can be cured with a few euros worth of antibiotics and disinfectant. Unfortunately, through lack of knowledge the diagnosis often comes too late. In just a few years, our Foundation would become the World Health Organisation's main partner in that field, financing the training of thousands of health care agents in several sub-Saharan African countries. The aim would be to provide each village with someone able to detect the very first symptoms of noma; at this stage the disease can still be cured. We hoped to eradicate that horrendous illness, which strikes mercilessly while the rest of the world remains indifferent.

For us, pushing on at 140 mph towards a glorious landing, there was no more 'rest of the world'. There was only one terrestrial globe, an immense hope which had just materialised, and our determination to devote our success to children who suffer, in order to give back a little of the luck we had been blessed with. As a tribute to what had made our success possible, this new foundation could only be called 'Winds of Hope'. Determination alone is not always enough to change the course of things. We need hope, because hope is what gives us the necessary humility to accept the profound meaning of the winds of Life. It may be that after our landing in the Egyptian desert, a new launch would enable us to make our modest contribution to what our era needs so badly: a bit more respect and compassion.

After an exhausting but happy twenty-first night, the last sunrise lit our capsule. As usual, the portholes had condensed the moisture from our breathing and were covered with a layer of morning frost. But this time, the sun was falling directly onto the window and made every ice crystal go through thousands of reddish iridescent shades. Behind the ice, which had caused us so many headaches for the first 20 days, the light was now shining. Beyond the failures, we had reached success at last. Doubts, anguish and our fear of the unknown had given way to intuition, trust and the spirit of adventure.

In life too, we often get iced up, and, sometimes, the layer can be so thick that it blocks out the light. We then feel lost and no longer know in what direction we should look for it. Problems can then become so insuperable, the suffering can get so bad that, caught up in the vagaries of the winds of life, we suddenly lose the ability to know if there is any light at all.

During the last three weeks we had been able to live our greatest adventure, but as we looked at our porthole, it was clear that the greatest adventure of all didn't lie in our victory, it didn't even lie in the first stratospheric flight, the dive to the Mariana Trench, the ascent of Everest or the conquest of the Moon. The greatest adventure suddenly seemed to be the breaking of the ice to reach the light. In that journey, convictions, certainties, dogmas, are all dead weight and an impediment to go through the obstacle. Our fear of the unknown, our need for control and power often make us stay where we are and endure the ice rather than make a move and take some risks to find the light.

It's a long and difficult path, but we do have some allies, the doubts and question marks brought by the turbulence and stormy winds of existence. If we try to resist them, the ice will get even thicker and our suffering will never end. But if we accept them, we'll be able to use them to stimulate our imagination and creativity, and find other solutions, other visions of the world, other levels of understanding. It's the only way we can stop resisting and start changing altitude to find another path. Admittedly, those are not the most pleasurable times in life; and such changes only take place if we are forced to seek them. In a sense, evolution is a difficult process which can only be carried out through crises; we have to crack the ice to see the light. Every time some ice darkens our horizon, we have to decide whether we want to regard it as one more problem meant to destroy us, or, as an opportunity to find within ourselves new resources and new behaviours which will enable us to take hold of our destiny.

But there are men, women and children who don't have the means to walk along that path, who don't even live at subsistence level and who cannot use the winds of Life. They have to struggle every day to survive hunger, war and oblivion.

If people are in a position to consider the meaning of their life, they also have the responsibility to help the weakest to do the same. They must sculpt in the ice of their existence some small openings that will enable them to find in which direction the light comes from. Only then will the 'spiritual world and the human world harvest the fruits of great achievements'.

Whatever the achievements and at whatever level, in the winds of Life, in the winds of Hope...

ECOMANITY
Curiosity, perseverance, respect

As we crossed the finish line, the director of the National Air and Space Museum in Washington, a member of the prestigious Smithsonian Institute, called the flight control centre to ask for the capsule of our balloon. He wanted to exhibit it in the hall devoted to historic big firsts, along with the Wright Brothers's aeroplane, Charles Lindbergh's *Spirit of St. Louis*, Chuck Yeager's supersonic X-1 and the Apollo 11 capsule in which Armstrong, Aldrin and Collins travelled to the Moon.

A few months later, Brian and I went to this extraordinary museum to rediscover *Breitling Orbiter 3*, sitting imposingly among the strange and marvellous aircraft flown by my child-hood heroes. I suddenly felt transported back to the days when I was a candid and naive 12-year old boy dreaming of becoming an explorer. A surge of emotion overtook me; it was like a release after 30 years of hopes… and doubts. Although it was stimulating, it was also very hard to be subjected to so many personal expecta-tions without knowing if destiny would enable me to fulfil them. I so often wondered if I wasn't setting my standards too high, if I wasn't risking everything.

That was the precise instant when the journey truly ended. The one around the world, of course, but above all, that first journey around life which I had been so keen to undertake. The dozen or so cameras focused on my face to catch its every reaction prevented me from properly enjoying the intensity of the moment. But there was something which no camera could capture: nobody could see that I was holding by the hand that little boy I had been, that little boy so eager to discover where the trace of his life would lead him. It was one of those magical moments when you manage to recreate within yourself, only more vividly, the sensations of consciousness you experienced in the past. I had found another piece of Ariadne's thread.

As a child I had thought that everything had been achieved, that there was no room for other big firsts. Now I knew this was totally wrong. There is always something new to be accomplished because the history of exploration must continue. Human imagination knows no bounds. Although in the future, things are likely to take place on another level. In fact, even before the *Breitling Orbiter 2* episode, I could already sense where the trace I was following would lead me. The press had spoken so much of the balloon trip around the world as the last big adventure that I had started to dream again. Then an idea had struck me; it was something so obvious that I would get on with it as soon as the time was right.

Now that Earth, Sea and Space have been conquered, the centuries where speed, duration and power counted are behind us. Our priorities have changed and we have other ways of making future generations dream. The aims will necessarily be different since the planet has already been explored extensively. We need to use human creativity and the spirit of adventure to improve the quality of life which present and future generations are entitled to. I think that future adventures will be humanitarian ones, to eradicate extreme poverty; political ones, to improve the governance of the planet; spiritual ones, to recover deep values without getting entangled in reductionist dogmas; medical ones to prevent new epidemics; and technological ones, to solve environmental threats while avoiding any type of ecological fanaticism.

That was precisely where I felt I was being led, and the success of Breitling Orbiter was going to provide the means to this end.

A 'change of altitude' in all these fields is imperative if we want to reverse the catastrophic course we have embarked on and which will lead us all to disaster.

We cannot continue pillaging in just a few decades the natural resources which took millions of years to form; nor can we contaminate and destroy our habitat so carelessly and short-sightedly. 'Changing altitude' implies a move towards sustainable development, accepting the technological challenge of renewable energies. At a political level, it means improving our government's ethics, overcoming sterile political divisions, finding new ways of progressing in the same direction: encouraging individual responsibility without neglecting social responsibility, and avoiding the obvious abuse on both sides. At an international level, it would mean altering the relationship between the countries who have everything and those who have nothing. I'm not talking about taking money from the rich to give it to the poor, no. Experience has shown that this just ends in generalised poverty. I'm talking about sharing potentials, of sharing opportunities of access to education, health and basic technology. This change is in fact a priority if we want to reduce all the tensions in the world; apart from being ethically unacceptable, they are also extremely dangerous for the balance of the planet and the evolution of mankind.

The security measures adopted by northern countries will soon be useless against the despair of those who have nothing to lose because, for a long time they have had nothing at all. Even in rich countries, there is a neglected underprivileged subsociety which grows by the day because of the stupid short-term vision of arrogant people who reckon they know what they're doing. Do we want everywhere to end up like Sao Paulo, where those with a few belongings have to barricade themselves behind electrified gates? On which side would freedom be?

Our political and financial leaders should pay more attention to the suffering of the destitute. Compassion may be the most important and, at the same time, the most difficult change to be brought about. If they had a loftier vision, they would understand that it is in their own interest. The world has become more sensitive. Gone are the days when heroes were ruthless conquerors. I think that historically speaking, what will essentially be remembered of the 21st century is the role played by those who endeavoured to promote more justice and balance, who cared for the well-being of the weak, for human rights and the protection of the environment. To 'change altitude' isn't a utopian or idealistic concept but a very specific process which aims at introducing the necessary modifications for the winds of life to push us in another direction, to get us out of the deadlock and suffering. Preaching in favour of humanism as an argument to get votes will soon be a major component of political programmes. But only those who understand this first will benefit.

The trip around the world in a balloon enabled me to express my views on these topics, to share some of my thoughts during my meetings with heads of states or during the hundreds of lectures I gave. Sometimes with a measure of success. When we met for the second time, the president of the Republic of Niger told me:

"The first time you came to see me, I didn't know what noma was, let alone that it affected my country…"

And he added this disease to the list of health priorities in Niger, along with AIDS and malaria. This is why Winds of Hope grew, to the point of financing the totality of the national programs against noma in Niger, Burkina-Faso, Mali, Benin, Togo and Senegal.

But speeches and audiences are not enough to bring about a remarkable difference. I now want to go even further.

I had noticed the public's enthusiasm for great adventures; I had seen how people identified with pioneers' and explorers' dreams. I decided that the new project I wanted to launch has enough potential to mobilise this enthusiasm and use it to promote the 'change of altitude' I have just mentioned. My project is challenging enough to stir emotions whilst remaining feasible, and it falls within the category of major firsts with direct consequences for society.

The idea is to rewrite the epic of aviation, but with solar energy. To design and build an aeroplane that can fly day and night thanks to this free and inexhaustible source of energy, thus approaching the mythical notion of perpetual flight. After a repetition of the main firsts of the past, such as the crossing of the Mediterranean, the United States and the Atlantic, the project will end with a trip around the world without fuel or toxic fumes.

Solar aeroplanes already exist, but their flight has always been limited to the maximum hours of sunshine. Paul MacCready's *Solar Challenger* did manage to cross the Channel. Unfortunately, the short range of these machines has reduced their history to a mere anecdote. They didn't have the technological capacity to accumulate enough energy for long flights, something which would have caught the public's attention.

We would therefore have to concentrate on that aspect in order to fulfil the crucial part of the dream: a 36-hour flight including one full night. Once this was done, there would be no limits.

Many designers gave up at that stage, the difficulty was too great. So why should I have a go at it? Maybe because one of the main things I learned as a child is that everything, or almost everything, is possible if you keep on trying. And if you have a good team. For me this project is the quintessence of my learning: without curiosity, you never get to do anything new; without perseverance, you never succeed in what you do; without respect, your success is meaningless.

I approached the École Polytechnique Fédérale de Lausanne, one of the top 4 universities in Europe, to request them to assess the feasibility of the project. Their positive conclusions were to have a decisive impact on my future.

The head of research, Stefan Catsicas, set up a nine-month interdisciplinary study which formed the bases of the project. It was co-ordinated by André Borschberg, an engineer and former fighter pilot, who eventually became my partner in the project.

In November 2003, we made it official: it would be called *Solar Impulse*. The news was received with great enthusiasm, as expected, and also some criticism from people who insinuated that I wanted to be in the limelight again. However, the most amazing question, one which I hadn't expected at all, and which I heard many times, was:

'Why are you embarking on a new adventure when you could rest on your laurels and live off your balloon flight?'

It just shows what our world is like! People prefer to keep still in case they fail, they don't try to progress, they forget that life offers no respite… It is true that many people don't try to fulfil their dreams in fear that they may be disappointed. Yet, as Jacques Brel used to say:

'So many men are burdened with the dreams they never accomplished.'

As far as I am concerned, I've always preferred to try and do things even if I failed rather than spend the rest of my life wishing I'd had the guts to do them.

Admittedly, *Solar Impulse* is a vast project, literally and figuratively. The study revealed that the aeroplane would need a 270 ft wingspan to meet with the aerodynamic requisites for a night flight, which would consume the energy accumulated in the batteries during the previous day. We needed top specialists to build carbon fibre wings of that size and rigid enough for the aeroplane to be manoeuvred properly. Not to mention the design of engines, propellers, a pressurised cockpit and some ultra-thin photovoltaic cells.

A year and a half after the announcement, the team exists and I admire its pioneering spirit. It is composed of some 50 members and more than 100 external advisers, all supervised by André.

Another encouraging thing is that several sponsors believed in the project from the beginning. Not enough to cover the totality of it, but enough to build the prototype. Solvay became the first of our four main sponsors. Next came Omega. Deeply involved in sustainable development through the Hayek family and its investments in electric cars, it had already supported Peter Blake's ecological expeditions. And it seemed only natural to wear, in Solar Impulse, the same watch as Armstrong and Aldrin on their journey to the Moon!

Deutsche Bank became our third major partner. This was an obvious asset for a project wanting to show the importance of the interface between ecology and economy. Through its investments in renewable energy and its advice in corporate social responsibility, Deutsche Bank is our access to the financial world. Altran Technology joined us as an engineering partner specialising in the management of complex systems, just like Semper, a Genevan investment company and Victorinox, the manufacturers of the Swiss knife which my grandfather, my father and I took on all our expeditions. Without forgetting, of course, the EPFL, our official scientific adviser, Dassault Aviation, our aviation adviser, and the European space agency, for transfers of technology.

Our friendship with Solvay is a long story. In the 1920s, Ernest Solvay invited all the major scientists of his time to scientific meetings. Several photos taken during these encounters show my grandfather with Albert Einstein and Marie Curie, amongst others. As time went by, this Belgian firm, a leader in numerous composite materials and other polymers, has remained faithful to its spirit of innovation.

After my success with the trip around the world, I often laughed when company directors told me that they would have loved to be in Breitling's place if I'd approached them. I don't believe a word of it. They would probably have refused, with the excuse that this type of adventure didn't fit with the usual marketing patterns. Those are usually limited to cultural or specific sports events, which can be exploited over a determined period of time. Before you can add your name to history books, you also have to 'change altitude' and take a risk with novelties. The more daring you are, the greater the reward.

Moreover, in the case of *Solar Impulse*, our sponsors committed themselves to a long-lasting project. Their long-term vision proves their credibility and sincerity. Adopting the values of the project, such as innovation, exploration, creativity, renewable energy, sustainable development, also demonstrates their interest in the real challenges which mankind has to face.

Every time I embark on a new project, the task seems insuperable. There are so many pitfalls, so many errors to avoid, so many problems to solve. Sometimes I wonder why I complicate my life so much. I'm not addicted to action, I would like to spend more time reading a book by the fireplace. Besides, my life style and my responsibilities put me on the margins, as in my teenage days. In the past, I studied my behaviour and my reactions with my hang glider instead of going out to the disco with my friends. Today I fear that I am distancing myself from those I love by my travels to the far corners of the world.

I hope that my true friends will understand. Still, I feel a bit nostalgic about those rare moments I spend with them, like that flight in a hot-air balloon on a misty morning in Tuscany, when they were able to share my passion.

My life is much as I dreamed it would be as a child – fascinating, but I have to accept the associated difficulties. Our society has two extremes – idealisation and denigration. For this reason, it often places its heroes on a higher pedestal than they're worth and later to bring them down to a lower level than they deserve. As soon as you become famous, you can make yourself heard, but you cannot afford to make the slightest error. You are judged by people you don't know, and who take the liberty to make comments out of context. Moreover, you are criticised for doing things which are seen as perfectly normal in others. There is a saying about having to live in hiding in order to live well. But if you want to influence things it seems to me that this is not the best way.

Yet, this is the type of life I have been attracted to ever since I marvelled at the Apollo rockets setting off for the Moon and made the wish to be an explorer. Actually, when I look back at things, my first day at school when I was 7, my first declaration of love when I was 14, and, later, my medical exams or my first loop, also seemed insuperable to me. The trip around the world showed me that we shouldn't be afraid of failure and that we have to keep on trying until we succeed. So why should I hesitate to embark on a greater adventure?

However, my worries about the future of the planet make me feel different from most of the people I mix with everyday. I'm afraid of being a kind of prophet of doom or spoilsport unable to fully enjoy the advantages of this world.

I have to say that my career as a doctor prompted me to study everything which can improve the quality of life. My relatives also set an example. Before my father's dives in a bathyscaphe, dumping chemical or radioactive waste in ocean trenches was regarded as reasonable. How could they rise from such an extreme depth? When they found a fish 36,000 ft below the sea, my father and his team mate, Don Walsh, demonstrated that between the surface and the bottom of the sea there was a descending current of oxygen, necessarily coupled with a counter-current which then went back returning to the surface. This expedition played a crucial role in the protection of nature, since from then onwards the seabed was no longer used as an official dump site.

When he returned from his Gulf Stream exploration, my father created a foundation for the study and protection of seas and lakes, and the first European ecology institute. But he was ahead of his time. Before it existed officially, ecology was misunderstood, and nobody took the problem seriously. Later, it developed into a kind of trend, but it became so highly politicised that people were put off. Nature is all too often used for partisan interests by fanatical movements. The green Khmers produced the opposite effect from that originally intended. They divided instead of uniting, they threatened people's mobility and attacked the functioning of society, without offering any satisfactory solution. What counters their argument is the fact that the industrial era has brought spectacular improvements and comfort, something which very few people are prepared to give up.

However, they are right in saying that the price we pay for our comfort is enormous. Our world consumes about one million tons of oil every hour, not to mention the other types of fossil fuels. The amount of toxic substances released in to the atmosphere is enough to disturb the climate. Half of mankind is left stagnating in unacceptable living conditions. But despite the crude reality, few of us hesitate between a model of society regarded as utopian and the mobility and daily comfort we basically need.

Unfortunately, as people's positions crystalize these topics become a source of confrontation. Between ecology and industry, solidarity and personal interests, left and right-wing political parties, in the same way as spirituality opposes everyday life. We never get anywhere, each side anihilating the other and we don't realise that it's in the itegration of extremes that we find solutions in which $1 + 1 = 3$.

Back in 1986, the Brundtland report requested by the UN dealt with the notion of sustainable development. It tried to find a way for the present generations to fulfil their needs without preventing future generations from doing the same. The study concluded that we had to quickly establish a balanced relationship between financial interests, ecology, and social responsibility.

Yet, we are still far removed from the concept of durability. Despite many grandiloquent speeches, the position seems to be in a deadlock because people too often associate durability with crippling expenses and restrictions in their comfort and mobility. This has to change. It is obvious that pollution and the waste of energy and raw materials can only lead mankind to destruction. But it is equally obvious that people aren't going to change the way they live unless they have something to gain straight away. It would be totally unrealistic to think that more than an insignificant amount of the population is prepared to swap cars for bicycles, to willingly pay more for renewable energy, or for environmentally friendly products. Nobody wants to see his standard of living drop, even if his behaviour is likely to destroy the planet. Our grandchildren will probably run out of petrol before the end of their life, they will then refer to us as the 'looters of raw materials'. Perhaps it is natural for human beings to be more motivated by short-term personal interests than by long-term compassion for future generations or for the environment.

If so, there is no point in trying to change the human nature, the battle is already lost. It would be like flying against the wind in a balloon. Let's take advantage of human nature and make use of its selfish and short-sighted vision of the world. Let's try and give people an immediate and specific personal interest in sustainable development. Let's show them how much money they could earn, how many jobs they could create. Let's demonstrate that this is a new and fantastic market with many financial and political outlets, new products, new production methods or saving energy, new ways of recycling rubbish. Let's also demonstrate that all this will exclusively benefit those who are clever enough to invest in time. As usual, only forerunners will have their fair share of the cake, unlike those who are too slow to react. We must show the scientific advantages of sustainable development, we have to promote the pioneering spirit, to enhance a new trend, in the positive meaning of the term, which will cause the users of renewable energy to be treated with admiration. Instead of forcing people to follow the way set in Rio de Janeiro or Kyoto, let's bring to the forefront all those who invent or use environment-friendly technologies. This way, consuming too much petrol, heating or cooling buildings in excess, using too many non-recyclable products, will soon become unfashionable or plainly unpopular.

A quick calculation by the Hong Kong environment minister showed me that the public authorities and private bodies of the city waste three billion US dollars a year, simply because they insist on cooling offices down to 59°F instead of maintaining a temperature of 77°F. Polluting is expensive, even on a short-term basis. When you consider the quality of Japanese cars based on a hybrid system of propulsion which combines an electric engine and an internal combustion engine, thus reducing fuel consumption by half, you can start fearing for the future of the European car industry. As for American cars, another rise or two in the price of petrol and nobody will want to buy them!

Sustainable development has to be backed by a genuine promotional and marketing policy. If they want to be heard, ecologists must speak the language of those they are trying to convince. We urgently need to abandon the sterile divisions maintained over the past 40 years. We have to make ecology and economy, environmental and financial interests, global vision and immediate political advantages, compatible at last.

All these examples just show that, graphically speaking, the circle of ecology is not necessarily in total opposition to the circle of economy. They may have an area in common, an intersection, and this intersection is what must be enhanced and developed, rather than waste time promoting one circle and neglecting the other.

This is why we are beginning to hear about market ecology. There are already a few good examples of industrials making their fortune in products or manufacturing methods which are environment-friendly. What we need is a new word to promote this spirit within the general public. People would identify with a new word which summed up the fact that lasting development is in their own interest, that the protection of the environment can be carried out without incurring an ecological fanaticism, that individual initiative goes hand in hand with social responsibility, that trade, finances and politics are more fruitful if they are ethical, that respect is not an old-fashioned moral value, that one can be spiritual without relying on religious dogmas. A term which would combine ecology, economy and humanism. 'Ecomanity', for example.

In this sense, *Solar Impulse* is an 'ecomanitarian' project.

But whatever its technical success, it will only be truly successful if it is acknowledged by both ecologists and financial circles. Having to abandon the plane and jump with a parachute isn't be the worst thing that could happen to me. The worst failure would be if industry took me for an 'eco-freak' while ecologists took me for a business man; if the right took me for a leftist while the left took me for a capitalist.

I would like *Solar Impulse* to be a rallying project, for exploration and scientific innovation to contribute positively to sustainable development. I would like it to produce positive feelings about renewable energy. People must know that they have to make important changes to safeguard the future of the planet in terms of ecology and energy. We have to turn the protection of the environment into something attractive, we have to show that, against all odds, alternative sources of energy combined with new technologies can provide solutions to what appear to be insoluble problems.

Solar Impulse isn't merely an aeroplane designed to go around the world without any fuel, it is intended to be a platform of communication centred on this topic. We want to mediatize the opinion of specialists and create information and educational networks, to bring together all those who believe that the future of the planet is linked to the development of new technologies rather than the constraints imposed by a reduction in transports and in the quality of life. All the communications relating to the different missions will be created within in this framework.

I know it's a symbolic gesture; we are unlikely to see the day when 300 passengers can be transported thanks to photovoltaic cells. But it is a gesture which affects everybody. We are all on Earth, and facing the same situation as the *Solar Impulse* pilot. If he doesn't use the right technology or if he wastes energy, he will have to land before the sun reappears. If we don't invest in the right scientific means to develop new sources of energy, or to use the energy we dispose of in a more rational way, we will go through a major crisis and won't be able to safeguard the planet for the next generations.

THE CENTRE

Between Earth and Sky

THERE WILL BE NO CONCLUSION TO THIS BOOK, since life is forever open. Finishing on a full stop would be like limiting the future. It would mean that I have become rigid in my beliefs, that I don't foresee a change in my views. In fact, life makes me change faster than I can express it; so much so, that I hardly dare write things down. I even see the past transform itself before my eyes, under every stroke of the pen, because, with time, events take on a different meaning. Although I was so certain about things in the past, I now see that what matters aren't the facts in themselves but whether I follow the same direction as the current of Life, or not. And this Life, which we only perceive during privileged moments of our existence, cannot be fixed in time or space, it doesn't even take on a specific form. We are the ones who become rigid in our beliefs, even though we only ever have a partial view of any situation.

I have often put pen to paper to express oppositions, contradictions: between science and intuition, between public life and introspection, between the human world and the spiritual realm. I even thought that I had to choose between family tradition and medicine. I didn't know then that, sometimes, medicine is not only a profession but also a way of exploring Life. Why aren't we taught about Paracelsius at university? According to him:

"The physician has been appointed by God to tell man what he is like, what restrains him or binds him, and what frees him", and also:

"He who publicly reveals the miracles of God is a physician (because) medicine, as the art of the physician, does not arise from the physician but from God".

All in all, there is no clear separation, no cleavage or opposition between the different aspects of our existence unless we stick to a temporary truth. In nature, everything moves; circles exist, infinite straight lines don't. And we are carried by these circles.

While reading my manuscript again, while bringing some changes to it in order to stick to the reality of the moment and to dare publish it at last, I could hear Josée de Salzmann teach the exercises she had learned from G.I. Gurdjieff:

"Don't become static; life is never static!"

Now that I realise how right she was, I also realise how rigid I was when I felt certain about metaphysical facts, how dogmatic I was even in my rejection of dogmas and how I isolated myself in an attempt to be open-minded, instead of listening to the emotions, to the ideas that flowed. Ideas are probably of secondary importance in the course of things; what matters is how you apply them. Once they are all put together, they belong to Life, without any opposition or contradiction. They are just perceived or applied differently, whether by following a trace in the field of science, medicine, in the sky or anywhere else in fact.

To think that for a long time I took my research to be incompatible with the family legacy! For years I studied the Taoist approach whereby human beings are the link between the sky and the earth, without paying attention to the title of the second book which my grandfather had written about the stratosphere: *Between Earth and Sky*. In fact, almost as if to underline such extremes, the commemorative coin minted by the Swiss Confederation showed the bathyscaphe and the stratospheric balloon placed opposite one another in the Yin Yang sign. In his own way, my grandfather had also been a link between above and below; he had also accomplished man's mission according to Taoism. When he said that balloons allowed him to live his adventures like a kind of sport for scientists, I can see that aviation made me discover sports like a kind of adventure for psychiatrists. All in all, it doesn't matter under what shape we carry out our investigations. Forms are called to change and eventually disappear, but the experiences we go through leave a trace on the earth, in the sky, and above all inside us.

This was also true of that superb weekend in March when I took part in a Chi Kung course at the foot of the Rochers-de-Naye, which I had so often used as a take-off site. Under a sky peppered with hang gliders and paragliders, I learned the posture and movements of the 'Flight of the Crane' which allow you to harness and distribute inside you the Chi, or vital energy. At some stage, at a moment offered by life, the crane takes off; the energy is liberated in your body and flows through your arms which are leaning on the air. I experienced the same lucidity, the same inner calm, the same clarity of mind as during my most beautiful flights; but I no longer needed a hang glider or a balloon to transcend the magnificent sight of the sunset over the lake. As I left the mountain at night, I still had this sensation of serenity which had marked my privileged encounters with the sky. In the end, what a friend had once told me was very true:

'One day, you won't need the hang glider anymore, you'll see.'

Again, I didn't feel that I was doing anything very different, but I was doing it at another level, as if continuing with my life while composing it in a more symbolical and subtle way. I felt as if I was pursuing the same research, but under a different, clearer light; and I wasn't flying alone, I was within a group and could share the experience. The circle revolved, and I was beginning to perceive the centre of it.

This means that I could have written this book in any other way, that I could have spoken about anything, and the final result would have been the same. If I hadn't seen a hang glider fly after coming back from the United States, if I hadn't met Hermann Geiger and Wernher von Braun, I could have begun Ariadne's Thread with: ' if the influence the sea has had over the first years of my life could be measured in pages, this chapter would take up most of the book...' And it would probably have been true. I would have mentioned my passion for diving, some anecdotes about submarines, my friendship with Jacques Mayol well before he was known as the Deep Blue, two crossings of the Atlantic in a liner, and everything I felt during a round of the Maxi yacht world championship. Above all, I would have talked about that night when I was fishing in Florida, caught up in a storm and drenched to the skin, and during which I discovered how to communicate with Nature.

The meaning of my message would have been the same if I had started it with: 'If the influence music has had over me...' I would have talked about my mother, a musician who brightened up the house every time she played the piano, about the silent tears I wiped off her face while she was listening to a Bach concerto, about her last Christmas, spent in hospital. I would also have mentioned all the different types of music which are recorded in my memory and which I associate with major events in my life.

I went back to Florida, to reactivate my childhood memories; I found the places and the friends I hadn't seen again since my return to Switzerland, except in my dreams. I walked along the channel from where the mesoscaphe had departed to explore the Gulf Stream, but this time I ran on the dike with my daughters. I visited Cape Kennedy and the Apollo launching sites again, but shuttles had replaced the Saturn V rockets and the conquest of the Moon had given way to routine journeys to space. I also went back to my school, and to my house; I wanted to see it all again to find out if something had changed, or rather to find out what had changed within me. Delving back into that intense period of my life stirred up a lot of emotions; however, I noticed for the first time that I wasn't nostalgic about things experienced during childhood but about the inferior state I was in when I lived them. It was like watching my life gyrate before my eyes and feel moved only by what was at the centre. In their explanations, psychoanalysts only go back to our nostalgia for the beatitude of the fusion between mother and child. In my case, it seemed that nostalgia was no longer related to childhood, but to something older, stronger, deeper and more subtle even than the visible side of life. As if there existed a state in which even the major events of life don't matter anymore, a state in which the passing of time no longer counts, but where the centre of life's circle suddenly becomes perceptible. In a flash of Consciousness, our whole Being is then filled with a familiar sensation of harmony. And it was the quest for that centre, for that sensation, which I had always pursued unwittingly, prompted by a feeling of nostalgia, without which I might have been satisfied with my material life. Like Ariadne's thread, nostalgia is the link which reminds us of what some would call the lost Paradise, the One or the Tao – nothing to do with the purity of childhood which I mentioned at the beginning of this book. All traditions mention this state which man once knew and which he sometimes remembers briefly during the privileged moments of his life.

I now understand why I've always liked Baudelaire and his inexplicable and unspeakable *Spleen*. I read about his nostalgia at a period when I was trying to soothe mine by stopping the flow of time under my hang glider. I was trying to slow down the rotation of the circle, but I couldn't see its centre, always motionless. Philosophies of all kinds hadn't been much use to me either, they all tended to deal with the circle rather than with its centre. My nostalgia was the only thing which had pushed me to search further away by following a trace in the sky.

I got to wonder whether nostalgia might not be a guide to prevents us from drifting too far away from the genuine state of consciousness which we probably knew before, and to which we must return some day; it is our responsibility. In fact, the word nostalgia means 'suffering caused by a burning desire to return'. How difficult it is to bear this suffering when all you notice is the passing of time!

When I came back from the trip around the world with my team mate, Estelle, Oriane and Solange rushed into my arms as fast as they could. My father came to greet us, just like my mother and I used to do when he came back from an expedition. Only in the meantime, I had become a father and he was a grandfather. When I shook my bunch of flowers under the ovation of thousands of people crammed on the runway at the airport, I had a thought for my father and my grandfather. They had broken all vertical records, upwards and downwards. As if to form a cross, I had added the horizontal record of the longest flight in history. The circle had gone round but it was still the same circle. I wondered what my father, in his eighties, felt about the circle having turned so much. I sincerely hoped that he perceived the centre as I did.

In fact, when I watch the people around me, I think that I wrote this chapter for them as much as for me. In this respect, writing can be a way of sharing and expressing love, as art and medicine ought to be.

For them, I could rewrite this book under the title 'Following a trace in Life' and make it start this way:

'Live from the earth':

I am very lonely in my research. Of course, this type of solitude encourages concentration, self-presence at all times, a certain form of meditation. But it also becomes one more obstacle in communication. When people ask me to tell them what the experience was like, I can only reconstruct it in snatches: I am no longer living it out. This is why, during my most intense experiences, I sometimes kept at the back of my mind a record of what I'd be saying later. One day, I felt the need to gather in a book all these impressions formed 'on the spur of the moment'. To share them and feel less lonely with my research.

In the different chapters, which unfold like 'tales about life', I sometimes hesitate to mention topics which are far removed from the preoccupations of everyday life. And what's worse, the very fact of using words may turn them into theories. Yet, there are so many of those already, that they become an impediment to spontaneous experimentation. Nevertheless, every idea, every theory, may become useful to try and define the Whole; all its facets put together form the integer of a prism. Every facet then becomes an opportunity to write a book, to develop a philosophy; but if we get obsessed with the construction of the prism, we end up forgetting the light which goes through it; we start neglecting the things which are directly perceptible through a developed intuition. Therefore, throughout my remarks, I've focused on the importance of receiving that light inside us. It is the only way to crystallise inside us those fleeting instants of Consciousness which we would like to be eternal.

Indeed, isn't our existence strewn with those privileged moments, those moments of grace when, through the sound of music, a gesture or a thought, the sudden sensation of connecting with our deep Being brings us to the centre of the big wheel of time.

This book has no other aim than to encourage the people I love to surpass their limits, not on earth, in the air or in the water, but within themselves, to find the centre of the circle of their own existence. If I have achieved it, then I will feel less lonely in my research…'

Photo Credits

Most of the illustrations come from the Piccard family archives.

My warmest thanks to all the photographers who allowed me to use their shots (listed in alphabetical order):

Archives Breitling
Christian Brustlein
Pierre Duperrex
Yvain Genevey
Claude Gluntz (*L'Illustré*)
Alain Guillou
Jean-Luc Iseli (*L'Illustré*)
Jules Verne Aventure
Jean-François Luy
Thierry Provost
Luca Ricchi
Schweizer Luftwaffe
Herb Swanson
François de Sury

And to those I haven't been able to trace back.